The National Labor Relations Board

Frank W. McCulloch
and
Tim Bornstein

PRAEGER PUBLISHERS
New York · Washington

Published in the United States of America in 1974
by Praeger Publishers, Inc.
111 Fourth Avenue, New York, N.Y. 10003

© 1974 by Praeger Publishers, Inc.

Library of Congress Cataloging in Publication Data
McCulloch, Frank W
    The National Labor Relations Board.
    (Praeger library of U.S. Government
departments and agencies)
    Bibliography. p. 193.
    1. United States. National Labor Relations
Board.   I. Bornstein, Tim, joint author.
KF3372.M23   353.008′3   73-10657

This book is No. 41 in the series
Praeger Library of U.S. Government Departments and Agencies

Printed in the United States of America

To
Edith and Barbara

Preface

In writing this book, we have felt the hand of history on our shoulders. It is the first work since the late 1940's to review the history of the National Labor Relations Board, the statutes it administers, its organization, procedures, and contributions to American industrial life. Our objective has been to provide the general reader with an overview of the Board in non-technical terms. Inevitably, we have sacrificed much detail that is important to the labor-law specialist, but there is no scarcity of technical treatises in law libraries.

Labor relations is a field that has always been intensely controversial. Since 1935, the NLRB has often been at the center of controversy, and much of the commentary about the work of the NLRB has had a partisan orientation. While there is no escaping the stubborn issues that divide labor and management, we have tried to sketch this portrait of the Board with balance and objectivity. We readily admit, however, to bias in favor of the broad congressional policies on which the Wagner and Taft-Hartley Acts rest.

While historians and economists might be quick to disagree, our judgment is that the system of participatory collective bargaining promoted by these statutes is, perhaps, the finest social invention of the twentieth century. It has softened the sharp, often brutal, edges of the Industrial Revolution and enriched political democracy by extending opportunities for self-determination to the daily lives of millions of Americans on the job.

Undoubtedly, our views about the Board have been influenced by our association with it during the 1960's. One of us (Frank McCulloch) served as its Chairman for nearly a decade and the other (Tim Bornstein) as his special assistant for two years. Although this book was written after our departure from the agency, we have ties of friendship and admiration for the men and women who serve the Board, whose careers have been dedicated to implementing policies of industrial democracy.

Among the major federal regulatory agencies, the NLRB is widely regarded as one of the most successful. It has been less lethargic than many old-line agencies that were established by Congress in a spirit of enthusiastic reform but that have long since been overwhelmed by timidity or silently captured by the interests they were created to regulate. Our historical review of the Board's institutional life demonstrates that it has responded with surprising vitality and energy to four decades of constant change in the workplace. Each new decade has thrown up novel legal issues for the Board to resolve within the broad framework of its statutory authority, and, in this sense, the NLRB has been required constantly to re-examine its function in our industrial society. It is apparent, nonetheless, that the Board has not realized its potential influence in bringing the labor-management community to accord on many basic issues.

The mistrust and hostility between labor and management that were characteristic of the 1930's have moderated over the years but have not been replaced by a guiding spirit of mutual trust and earnest cooperation. In Congress, before the NLRB, and at the bargaining table, zealous partisanship is still the rule; common concern for the public interest remains the exception. Today, nearly forty years after passage of the

Wagner Act, the Board is required to act as a policeman to halt patently lawless conduct by parties who only grudgingly obey the law.

The Board's course has too often been influenced by national political changes, and it has too often receded from inventive solutions to problems in the face of partisan criticism. Despite broad statutory power to fashion remedies for unfair labor practices, the Board in the wake of judicial setbacks has been reluctant to use this authority with either great vigor or imagination. Despite its unquestioned authority to rely on the results of external research to help it develop more sensitive and effective policies, the NLRB, preoccupied with its rapidly mounting work load, has largely overlooked the results of external research conducted by industrial-relations scholars.

Our over-all assessment is that the NLRB and the statutes it administers have been highly successful, despite formidable obstacles—but its successes have not been unqualified, and its future is constantly challenged by political and economic forces that oppose the national labor policy.

Many people deserve our gratitude for helping to bring this book to completion. John Truesdale, executive secretary of the NLRB, read the manuscript with a critical eye and mature insights. Lois O'Neill, Fred Howard, Joan Tapper, and Malinda Elliott of Praeger Publishers have been unfailingly helpful. And, finally, our families have carried with patience and good cheer the burden of our working vacations and working weekends.

FRANK W. McCULLOCH
Charlottesville, Virginia
TIM BORNSTEIN
Amherst, Massachusetts

January, 1974

Contents

List of Charts

List of Tables

A section of photographs follows page 84.

The National Labor
Relations Board

I

Before the Wagner Act

The enactment of the National Labor Relations Act of 1935, popularly known as the Wagner Act, culminated the struggle of more than a century over the right of workers to join unions of their choice and to engage in collective bargaining. It is a complex law. Over the years, it has undergone two major revisions by Congress, and its meaning has been clarified and refined by thousands of decisions of the National Labor Relations Board and the federal courts.

Like other landmark social legislation, the National Labor Relations Act was born in a period of national crisis, but its roots and the problems it was designed to solve lie deep in history.

LABOR RELATIONS FROM COLONIAL TIMES TO THE CIVIL WAR

The economy of colonial America was dominated by independent farmers, artisans, and shopkeepers, but, in fact, nearly half of the white immigrants to the colonies were indentured servants who pledged their services for a fixed number of years in exchange for ocean passage, room and board, and nominal wages. Colonial law greatly respected a master's "property" rights to the labor of his servants but gave

3

only limited protection to servants from cruel and oppressive treatment by their masters.

Tens of thousands of black immigrants came from Africa in chains, bound for life to do their owners' bidding with virtually no protection under the law. Their status was aptly described by the beautiful slave girl Cassy in *Uncle Tom's Cabin:* "There's no law here, of God or man, that can do you, or any one of us, the least good."

When America gained its independence in the late eighteenth century, powerful new economic forces were on the horizon. The craft workshop tradition was beginning to give way to a new and vastly more complex economic order—the factory system. Early in the nineteenth century, journeymen craftsmen, sensitive to the breakdown of traditional relations with their masters, formed local societies to protect their wage and piecework rates. They met with fierce resistance from their employers and the courts.

In the fall of 1805, a society of cordwainers (shoemakers) called a strike in Philadelphia to demand higher piecework rates. The strike lasted several weeks and ended in total failure, but it prompted the first labor-relations case in American history, the *Philadelphia Cordwainers* case of 1806. The strike leaders were charged with illegally conspiring to raise their wages. The mayor's court of Philadelphia found them guilty and ruled bluntly that it was a crime for workers to create a labor organization for the purpose of raising their wages and improving their working conditions. This ruling became known as the "criminal conspiracy doctrine."

Although legal scholars today believe that the foundation for this doctrine was spurious, nonetheless it accurately reflected the hostility of the courts toward the embryonic labor movement, a hostility that persisted well into the twentieth century. Several dozen strikes were broken by judges who invoked the criminal conspiracy doctrine in the following decades, but in a few notable instances juries stubbornly refused to convict workers of this crime, despite instructions from the judge. Some cases sparked mass protests.

By the 1840's, the courts lost confidence in the harsh criminal conspiracy doctrine, which made unions themselves illegal. Instead, a new and more subtle civil conspiracy doctrine gained currency. Now the courts held that it was not illegal for workers to form unions, provided that unions did not engage in strikes or otherwise interfere with an employer's production. Many courts were, nevertheless, quick to find that a union's "ends" were unlawful, even though its "means" were legitimate, while in other instances the courts would approve a union's "ends" but condemn its "means." The result in practical terms was much the same: Strikes and other forms of concerted labor activity were treated inhospitably by the courts.

FROM THE CIVIL WAR TO WORLD WAR I

The U.S. economy prospered, and labor became scarce during the Civil War, encouraging workers to join together to improve their lot. By the war's end, 200,000 workers had joined labor organizations, now called trade unions. The factory system had largely replaced handicraft workshops, and a new class of industrial workers was emerging. Local workingmen's societies of the pre-Civil War decades were succeeded by national labor unions that sought to match the growing economic power of great national corporations. This was the era of the short-lived National Labor Union and the equally ill-fated and quixotic Knights of Labor.

The 1870's and 1880's were crucial in the history of American industrial relations. Under the leadership of a formidable young cigar-maker, Samuel Gompers, the new American Federation of Labor (AFL) brought together a number of national craft unions to pursue a highly pragmatic approach to labor relations. Gompers called it "pure and simple" unionism, for it emphasized direct and immediate economic gains and avoided ideological commitment to long-range political movements. Its chief tactics were the strike and the consumer boycott.

During these decades, 8 million immigrants from Europe filled out the growing industrial work force of unskilled and semiskilled wage earners. They had no place in the AFL, which concerned itself only with the welfare of labor's "elite," the skilled craftsmen.

Strikes were becoming a familiar part of American economic life, and many were characterized by brutality and violence committed by both sides. This period witnessed the violent railroad strike of 1877, the brutal acts of the Molly Maguires in the 1860's and 1870's, and the Chicago Haymarket Square uprising and massacre of 1886. To deal with militant unions, employers began to experiment with tough tactics, including the use of professional strikebreakers, private police battalions, lockouts, blacklists, and the infamous "yellow dog" contract.*

The offices of government—legislators, executive officials, and, especially, the courts—were far from sympathetic to the growing labor movement. Judges were quick to convict trade unionists of crimes arising out of strike activity. And, with increasing frequency, the courts began to employ the most effective and hated method of judicial control of labor relations—the labor injunction. As an outgrowth of the Pullman strike of 1894, led by Eugene V. Debs's American Railway Union, the Supreme Court approved the labor injunction as "recognized from ancient times and by indubitable authority." Labor decried "government by injunction." Despite judicial repression, industrial turbulence persisted.

As the nineteenth century drew to a close, public attention was riveted on labor-management conflict, and a search began for long-term public policies to sort out the complex and

---

* A written pledge by a worker that he will not join a union during the period of his employment.

competing claims of the parties. It was a search for industrial democracy and for policies and procedures that would encourage mutual respect in the workplace and affirm the legitimacy of joint decision-making on the job.

As early as 1901, the U.S. Industrial Commission published a monumental study of the state of labor relations in America that, like the U.S. Strike Commission seven years before, pointed to the participatory procedures of collective bargaining as the essential foundation of a workable national labor policy. A third of a century would pass, however, before this recommendation would be accepted by Congress.

In the first two decades of the twentieth century, the labor movement was plagued not only by the use of the injunction but also by the application of the Sherman Antitrust Act to its activities. Congress had intended the Sherman Act to apply to business combinations, but the courts inventively found ways to turn Congress's words against labor activity. The courts likewise aborted the 1914 effort of Congress through the Clayton Act to erect a shield for labor against antitrust prosecutions. Labor remained on the defensive.

From World War I to the Great Depression

As America prepared to enter the "Great War" in 1917, labor scarcity and the need for labor-relations stability led President Wilson to create a tripartite War Labor Conference Board. Among its guiding principles were the prohibition of strikes and of lockouts and recognition of the "right of workers to organize in trade unions and to bargain collectively through chosen representatives." This was a remarkable declaration of labor's rights, and during its short life the board heard 1,250 cases affecting 700,000 workers. The impact of its work was temporary, however, for the spirit of labor-management harmony induced by the war did not survive the armistice in 1918.

Although labor looked forward to the postwar years with

promise, its hopes were soon frustrated. By the war's end, the AFL claimed over 5 million members; but, by 1923, its membership had declined by a million and a half. The steel strike of 1919, as well as major coal and rail strikes in that year, ended in failure. A new wave of management hostility in the form of the "American Plan"—essentially an antiunion, open-shop program—dominated the 1920's. And during this period the use of the labor injunction reached its zenith.

The only substantial success that labor could claim in this decade was the Railway Labor Act in 1926. But even passage of this legislation was only a qualified victory, for it was a weak compromise of provisions that had been agreed on by rail labor and management. Weak as it was, particularly because it lacked administrative machinery, the Act was a breakthrough for labor because it stressed the importance of collective bargaining in the rail industry. It declared, moreover, that representatives of the parties were to be chosen "without interference, influence, or coercion exercised by either party over the self-organization [of] the other." In simpler terms, Congress guaranteed the right of railroad workers to select their own bargaining agents free from employer interference.

Some remember the 1920's as a gay and golden decade, the "flapper" era, a carefree period of peace and general prosperity. But its finale was the stock market crash of October, 1929. The bubble of national self-confidence burst, and the nation plunged rapidly into the deepest, longest economic depression in its history.

The Great Depression of the 1930's had three major influences on the shape and content of labor-management policies: First, widespread unemployment shocked the country out of complacency about industrial conditions and created a climate in which Congress was willing to experiment with new approaches to labor relations. Second, the harshness of industrial life during this decade—particularly low wages and job insecurity—caused part of the labor movement itself to reach out to the long-ignored workers in the mass production industries. And, third, the fear of revolutionary social formulas from the Far Left and Right persuaded opinion-makers that meaningful reform in the workplace was essential to the maintenance of a democratic society.

Familiar unemployment statistics of the Depression give only a hint of the widespread human misery. Unemployment increased from 492,000 in October, 1929, to 4,065,000 the following January. And by January, 1931, more than 9 million workers were unemployed. Real wages fell precipitously as the length of the work week was cut in industry after industry.

The Hoover Administration talked optimistically about the essential soundness of the economy, but official and private economic indicators pointed to a worsening decline in jobs, earnings, and production.

Ironically, in 1932, the final year of President Herbert Hoover's term, when the entire economy and the labor movement had sunk to unprecedented depths, Congress passed the Norris–La Guardia Act, a federal anti-injunction statute that broadly curbed the power of federal courts to interfere with peaceful labor activities. This action was a response to public resentment over the indiscriminate use of the injunction by federal judges during the 1920's. Moreover, following Congress's example, many states enacted their own anti-injunction laws that similarly curbed judicial intrusions in peaceful labor-management disputes.

NEW DEAL LABOR POLICIES PRIOR TO THE WAGNER ACT

On President Franklin D. Roosevelt's inauguration day, March 4, 1933, one out of three American workers was unemployed. Countless others were underemployed. The new President declared in his inaugural address: "Our greatest primary task is to put people to work." The late Edmund Wilson wrote of this period that "the whole structure of American society seemed actually to be going to pieces."

During the famous Hundred Days following Roosevelt's inauguration, Congress followed his leadership in approving a number of innovative approaches to revive the economy. Surely the boldest of these was the National Industrial Recovery Act (NIRA), which swept through Congress on a tidal wave of urgency and was signed by the President on June 16, 1933. The scheme of the NIRA was to relax the antitrust laws to permit employers within a single industry to enter into cooperative codes of fair competition so as to increase employment, establish minimum wages and hours, and accelerate production and purchasing power. In effect, the Act permitted price-fixing in exchange for industry's willingness to maintain employment and agreed-on wage levels.

In order to encourage the labor movement's cooperation in the programs generated by the NIRA, the White House and Congress agreed to an obscure provision in that statute—Section 7(a)—patterned largely after the policy declarations in the Norris–La Guardia Act. On its enactment, labor leaders were quick to recognize Section 7(a) as the firmest expression in the nation's history of the right of workers to join unions and engage in collective bargaining. Some called it labor's Magna Charta. In substance, Section 7 (a) required every code of fair competition under the NIRA to include the following terms:

> (1) That employees shall have the right to organize and bargain collectively through representatives of their own choosing, and shall be free from the interference, restraint, or coercion of employers of labor, or their agents, in the designation of such representatives or in self-organization or in other concerted activities for the purpose of collective bargaining or other mutual aid or protection; (2) That no employee and no one seeking employment shall be required as a condition of employment to join any company union or to refrain from joining, organizing, or assisting a labor organization of his own choosing.

Although Section 7(a) was scarcely more than a declaration of policy, wholly lacking in administrative machinery for its enforcement, it seemed to have a remarkable energizing effect on the labor movement. In combination with other causes, Section 7(a) was a catalyst for a frenzy of organizing, employer resistance, and strike activity throughout the country. There were more strikes in the summer of 1933 than in the preceding two years combined.

In response to widespread labor unrest, President Roosevelt appointed a National Labor Board in August, 1933, to bring about compliance with Section 7(a) and to mediate labor disputes. As chairman of this board, the President named his old friend and ally Senator Robert Wagner of New York as the public member. Other members were named as representatives of labor and industry.

The National Labor Board had little real power and a dubious legal foundation as well. In December, 1933, the President issued an executive order to formalize the powers of the board. And in February, 1934, he issued Executive Order 6580, which authorized the board to conduct elections in which employees could freely select their own bargaining agents, to publish the results of these elections, and to deal with violations of the labor provisions of the codes.

Senator Wagner and his colleagues on the National Labor Board soon learned that most employers did not welcome their efforts. From labor's point of view, the weaknesses in the administration and enforcement of the NIRA codes were fatal. Some labor leaders called the National Recovery Administration, created by the NIRA—the NRA—the "National Run Around." In fact, the National Labor Board's sole power of enforcement was to report violations to the Compliance Division of the National Recovery Administration or to the Attorney General. The Compliance Division's sole authority was to withdraw the privilege of display of the NRA's symbolic "Blue Eagle" from a violator, scarcely a formidable deterrent.

Despite the administrative weaknesses of the National

Labor Board and despite wholesale management rejection of the principles of Section 7(a), a new mood of hope and confidence had been generated among the leaders of the labor movement. To them, Section 7(a) conveyed that the Roosevelt Administration was sympathetic to their aspirations. In hundreds of organizing campaigns, unions used Section 7(a) as the basis for telling unorganized workers: "President Roosevelt wants you to join the union!"

The National Labor Board pursued its work energetically during its life, which lasted less than one year: It settled 1,019 strikes, averted 498 others, and settled 1,800 other kinds of labor controversies. When its authority expired in July, 1934, its strengths overwhelmed by its weaknesses, it had cultivated the seedbed from which the Wagner Act was soon to grow.

Senator Wagner had been profoundly frustrated by the National Labor Board's inability to achieve voluntary compliance with Section 7(a). In response to this experience, he introduced a bill in the Senate on February 28, 1934, to prohibit employer "unfair labor practices" and to establish a permanent agency to administer its provisions. Wagner's bill (S. 2926) envisioned a tripartite agency, consisting of two employee, two management, and three public members. Hearings on this bill brought heavy attacks from management on its constitutionality and its fairness. When it soon became evident that the Wagner bill could not be passed in 1934, and in the face of a renewed national wave of strikes, Congress passed a joint resolution—Public Resolution No. 44—that authorized the President to establish one or more boards to investigate controversies arising under Section 7(a), to conduct representation elections, and to require witnesses to appear before them. It authorized, in other words, the creation of an agency only slightly stronger than the National Labor Board. And it, like the board, was to have a life of only one year, expiring on June 16, 1935.

Management regarded Public Resolution No. 44 as pretty

weak tea in comparison with Wagner's now doomed S. 2926. Accordingly, Congress adopted Resolution No. 44 without great controversy. As one U.S. Steel Corporation executive wrote, "My personal opinion is that it is not going to bother us very much."

Acting under Resolution No. 44, Roosevelt created a new body, the National Labor Relations Board, whose life began July 9, 1934. Unlike the tripartite National Labor Board, the new National Labor Relations Board was to be staffed by three public members. Roosevelt named as its first chairman the dean of the University of Wisconsin Law School, Lloyd K. Garrison. After several months, Garrison resigned and was replaced by one of the great lawyers of his time, Francis Biddle of Philadelphia, a distinguished corporation lawyer who was later to become Attorney General of the United States. The other members were Harry A. Millis, a prominent labor economist from the University of Chicago, and Edwin S. Smith, an obscure state official from Massachusetts.

Like the National Labor Board, the new National Labor Relations Board immediately discovered its inability to achieve voluntary compliance with the policies of Section 7(a). It mediated a number of disputes, nonetheless, conducted many elections, and had the Blue Eagle withdrawn from several dozen noncomplying employers. The board readily acknowledged in one of its reports, however, that it was "powerless to enforce its decisions."

If the National Labor Relations Board under Francis Biddle's leadership was administratively weak, it was incredibly energetic in giving substance and meaning to the vague contours of Section 7(a). It wrote a number of thoughtful decisions that later became an invaluable reservoir of sound labor-relations judgments for the second National Labor Relations Board created by the Wagner Act (described in the next chapter).

Foremost among the decisions of the first National Labor Relations Board, created by Resolution No. 44, was the

Houde Engineering Corporation case, which articulated the premises of "good faith" collective bargaining. For many years this decision has been regarded as a landmark, especially because of the following passages:

> The right of employees to bargain collectively implies a duty on the part of the employer to bargain with their representatives. Without this duty to bargain the right to bargain would be sterile; and Congress did not intend the right to be sterile. . . . The National Labor Board [has] established the incontestably sound principles that the employer is obliged by the statute to negotiate in good faith with his employees' representatives; to match their proposals, if unacceptable, with counter proposals; and to make every reasonable effort to reach an agreement. Collective bargaining, then, is simply a means to an end. The end is an agreement. And, customarily, such an agreement will have to do with wages, hours and basic working conditions, and will have a fixed duration. The purpose of every such agreement has been to stabilize, for a certain period, the terms of employment, for the protection alike of employer and employee. By contrast, where all that transpires is a demand by any employees for better terms and assent by the employer, but without any understanding as to duration, there has been no collective bargaining, because neither side has been bound to anything.

During the two years of the National Labor Board and the first National Labor Relations Board, 1933–35, the labor-relations picture had changed almost beyond recognition. Unions were growing at a dizzying speed: The United Mine Workers Union alone grew from 60,000 members in 1932 to over 300,000 by late 1933, and a quarter of all unions in the AFL doubled their memberships between 1932 and 1935. Much of their new membership came from the previously unorganized mass production industries. The reasons for this unprecedented growth were many and complex, but unquestionably the enactment of Section 7(a) of the NIRA was a vital spur.

Strike activity during these two years was also unprecedented. It has been estimated that in 1934 one-seventh of the national work force was involved in some form of industrial conflict. Nearly 125,000 workers struck at a single time in San Francisco as an outgrowth of a dispute that began with longshoremen. In September, half a million textile workers were on strike in twenty states.

Labor's new militancy was matched by determined management resistance. A New England textile industry journal, reflecting the dark mood of some employers during the textile strikes of 1934, wrote: "A few hundred funerals will have a quieting influence." And that popular, mythical figure of the 1930's, Mr. Dooley, commented that management's preference was for unions that had "no strikes, no rules, no contracts, no scales, hardly iny wages an' dam' few mimbers." As tens of thousands of workers were joining unions affiliated with the AFL, even more were joining company unions or so-called employee representation plans that were devised by employers to fend off outside organizations.

In May, 1935, the shaky edifice of voluntary codes created by the National Industrial Recovery Act collapsed. A fatal blow was struck by the Supreme Court in that month in the famous "sick chicken" case, *Schechter Poultry Corporation* v. *U.S.*, which declared the NRA unconstitutional. In reality, however, Section 7(a) had little life left when the Supreme Court sealed its doom. General Hugh Johnson, first administrator of the NRA, testified before the Senate Finance Committee in April, 1935: "I think section 7(a) has substantially failed of its original purpose."

While the Supreme Court in its austere chambers was writing the obituary for the NIRA, several thousand feet away in the Capitol, Congress was at work on a comprehensive new labor statute, the Wagner Act. And in plants, mines, and other workplaces throughout the economically depressed nation, restless workers were rallying to an invigorated labor movement.

II

The Wagner Act and
the Birth of the NLRB

The law that is generally known as the "National Labor Relations Act" is actually three separate statutes enacted by Congress at 12-year intervals: the Wagner Act of 1935 (officially titled the National Labor Relations Act), the Taft-Hartley Act of 1947 (officially the Labor-Management Relations Act), and the Landrum-Griffin Act of 1959 (the Labor-Management Reporting and Disclosure Act). Because the Taft-Hartley and Landrum-Griffin laws were in the nature of amendments to the Wagner Act, it is correct to refer to the single, combined law as the "National Labor Relations Act, as amended," or simply as the "Labor Act."

In each of these three statutes, Congress responded to powerful social, economic, and political forces of the moment. To understand the Labor Act and the work of the National Labor Relations Board (NLRB), which administers it, one must inevitably turn to their sources.

LEGISLATIVE HISTORY OF THE WAGNER ACT

In the congressional elections in November, 1934, an overwhelming Democratic majority was sent to Washington. This

Congress was committed to the policies of the New Deal and loyal to the leadership of Franklin Roosevelt. Both the mood of the country and the spirit of Congress were ripe for formulating long-term and fundamental national labor policies.

Senator Robert Wagner introduced his famous bill, S. 1958, on February 15, 1935, and despite its official title, it has borne the late New York senator's name for more than a generation.

Ironically, President Roosevelt would later take pride in the Wagner Act as one of the high achievements of the early New Deal, but, in fact, he was rather cool to Senator Wagner's bill until virtually the eve of its passage. Roosevelt preferred a more consensual statute, one that could be jointly agreed on by labor and management, like the Railway Labor Act of 1926.

Management opposition to the Wagner Act was fierce and unqualified. Senator Wagner, however, was a powerful figure in Congress, and he was determined to see his bill enacted with or without the blessing of the White House.

Hearings on Senator Wagner's bill in the winter and spring of 1935 were extensive in both houses of Congress. As could be expected, the unions supported it enthusiastically, citing in their testimony countless examples of management interference with the self-organizational rights of workers. And, just as predictably, management opposed the bill both in principle and in detail.

A spokesman for the Illinois Manufacturers' Association was typical of employer opponents. In testimony before the Senate Committee on Labor and Public Welfare, he said:

> We have had an opportunity to canvass the views of our members on the Wagner labor disputes bill and we are prepared to say that they are universally and unqualifiedly opposed to this measure. They regard the introduction of this bill at this time, when industry is making desperate efforts to provide employment and promote recovery, as distinctly unfortunate. They believe that the promotion of radical, ill-conceived legislation of this character tends to create apprehension and uncertainty on the part of productive enterprise and materially retards im-

provement in business conditions. They regard this bill as the most amazing attack upon the rights of employers and the great mass of workers that has thus far been devised.

Despite intense opposition from management and, perversely, from the Communist Far Left (which regarded the bill as a cruel "deception" of workers), Wagner's bill passed the Senate by a lopsided vote, sixty-three to twelve, on May 16, 1935. At this point, the White House publicly endorsed the bill for the first time, and it easily passed the House of Representatives by a voice vote on June 19. Insignificant differences between the Senate and House bills were easily resolved by a conference committee, and the agreed-on bill was overwhelmingly approved by the entire Congress in late June.

On July 5, 1935, without the pomp and ceremony that often accompany the signing of historic legislation, President Roosevelt quietly signed the National Labor Relations Act and issued a low-key message. It said, in part:

> A better relationship between labor and management is the high purpose of this act. By assuring the employees the right of collective bargaining it fosters the development of the employment contract on a sound and equitable basis. By providing for an orderly procedure for determining who is entitled to represent the employees, it aims to remove one of the chief causes of wasteful economic strife. By preventing practices which tend to destroy the independence of labor it seeks, for every worker within its scope, that freedom which is justly his.

Years later the historian James MacGregor Burns would write that the Wagner Act was "the most radical legislation passed during the New Deal, in the sense that it altered fundamentally the nation's politics by vesting massive economic and political power in organized labor."

MAJOR POLICIES OF THE WAGNER ACT

Although a remarkably short statute in terms of its ambitious scope, the Wagner Act contains some extremely broad passages, and some that are narrow and precise in meaning.

Because Congress's power to enact this law rested on the commerce clause of the Constitution, Section 1 of the law emphasizes Congress's finding that employer interference with the right of workers to organize and the refusal of employers to bargain collectively lead to industrial strife, which, in turn, burdens interstate commerce. With recent labor turmoil in mind Congress announced a new national labor policy:

> It is hereby declared to be the policy of the United States to eliminate the causes of certain substantial obstructions to the free flow of commerce and to mitigate and eliminate these obstructions when they have occurred by encouraging the practice and procedure of collective bargaining and by protecting the exercise by workers of full freedom of association, self-organization, and designation of representatives of their own choosing, for the purpose of negotiating the terms and conditions of their employment or other mutual aid or protection.

With this declaration, American history turned a corner—perhaps one of the most important since the Emancipation Proclamation. For millions of wage earners in every state in the nation, Congress had established an industrial bill of rights, acknowledging that in an industrial society democracy in the workplace is as important as democracy in politics.

Translating this sweeping declaration of industrial democracy into practical administrative terms required a high order of legal artistry. Moreover, of incalculable historical importance is the fact that, by passing the Wagner Act, Congress chose to shape labor relations and the institution of collective bargaining according to legal standards. By contrast, in other industrialized Western nations, notably in the Scandinavian countries and Great Britain, collective bargaining had come by voluntary acceptance, rather than by force of law. From 1935 forward, there has been no turning back from the statutory approach to collective bargaining, and ours has become an industrial-relations system regulated in large measure by legal prescription. Many scholars lament "excessive legalism" in the American system, but, in 1935, the die was cast, perhaps irrevocably.

The heart of the Wagner Act is Section 7, "Rights of Employees." The forty-one words of this section have been the subject of literally thousands of NLRB and court decisions, for Section 7 formulates the specific rights of workers that the new law would protect. The remainder of the statute was designed to implement these fundamental rights:

> Employees shall have the right to self-organization, to form, join, or assist labor organizations, to bargain collectively through representatives of their own choosing, and to engage in concerted activities, for the purpose of collective bargaining or other mutual aid or protection.

With the exception of the Bill of Rights of the United States Constitution, Section 7 of the Wagner Act has probably been more studied and litigated than any other single provision in American law. Each of its three primary components—the right of *self-organization,* the right to engage in *collective bargaining through freely chosen representatives,* and the right to engage in *concerted activities*—has been given specific meaning in an endless variety of factual situations.

The Wagner Act is divided into two major parts: employer unfair labor practices and employee representation elections.

Unfair Labor Practices

Five prohibitions against management were set forth in Section 8 of the Wagner Act to guarantee the rights of employees stated generally in Section 7. These prohibitions, called "unfair labor practices," deal only with employer conduct. (Not until the Taft-Hartley Amendments of 1947 would Congress define unfair labor practices for unions.)

Section 8(1). This first and broadest unfair labor practice provision forbade employers to "interfere with, restrain, or coerce employees in the exercise of the rights guaranteed in

Section 7." In Chapter VI, we shall review a number of the major decisions that have interpreted this omnibus unfair labor practice. In general, it prohibits management threats, surveillance, espionage, restrictions on employee solicitation and communication, and promises of benefit and violence. As the Supreme Court was later to observe, in *NLRB* v. *Stowe Spinning Company,* Congress left to the NLRB the job of applying this "general prohibitory language in the light of the infinite combinations of events which might be charged as violative of its terms."

Section 8(2). During the period of the National Recovery Administration, the problem of "company unionism"—unions created or supported by employers—was rampant. To assure that employees would be truly free to select legitimate unions of their choice, Section 8(2) provided simply that employers shall not "dominate or interfere with the formation or administration of any labor organization or contribute financial support to it."

Section 8(3). For decades prior to the Wagner Act, the classic response of antiunion employers to the union activities of employees was to discharge or otherwise punish them. Thus, Section 8(3) broadly prohibited "discrimination in regard to hire or tenure of employment or any term or condition of employment to encourage or discourage membership in any labor organization." No longer could employers say to union leaders and sympathizers: "You're fired for joining a union." Workers were also protected from discriminatory wage cuts, layoffs, reassignments to onerous jobs, and a host of other forms of job discrimination. A proviso to Section 8(3) authorized closed shops and other types of union security contracts.

Section 8(4). To guarantee access to the benefits of the statute, Section 8(4) provided that employers shall not "discharge or otherwise discriminate against an employee because he has filed charges or given testimony under this Act."

Section 8(5). The last unfair labor practice required employers "to bargain collectively" with the representatives of employees. In essence, this provision required employers to engage in good faith negotiations with a labor organization properly selected as the majority agent of employees. In some of its applications, this section has generated enormous controversy over the years.

Representation Elections and Related Policies

In Section 9 of the Wagner Act, Congress laid down three extraordinary concepts that have been widely accepted in our labor-relations system:

Section 9(a). If a representative has been selected by a majority of employees in an appropriate unit, such a representative becomes the "exclusive representative of all the employees in such a unit for the purposes of collective bargaining in respect to rates of pay, wages, hours of employment, or other conditions of employment." This provision had two major purposes: First, it spells out the notion of exclusive representation, which simply means that a majority union must represent *all* employees in a bargaining unit. Congress flatly rejected proportional representation among various unions, a pattern common in England and elsewhere. Second, Congress defined the subject matter of collective bargaining in general terms of wages, hours, and other conditions of employment. As we shall see in later chapters, these provisions have had broad ramifications over the years.

Section 9(b). In this section, Congress defined the concept of an "appropriate bargaining unit," and it directed the NLRB "to decide in each case whether, in order to insure to employees the full benefit of their right to self-organization and to collective bargaining . . . , the unit appropriate for the purposes of collective bargaining shall be the employer unit, craft unit, plant unit, or subdivision thereof." To put it simply, Congress directed the NLRB to prescribe voting districts for employees in industry. The importance of the bargaining unit concept is that only employees within the approved unit may vote in representation elections, and, moreover, the employer's obligation to bargain is limited to employees in that unit. The task of devising appropriate bargaining units has been one of the NLRB's most burdensome and controversial responsibilities.

Section 9(c). Once the NLRB has determined the voting unit, Congress provided that employees would vote in secret-ballot elections or by "any other suitable" means to decide whether they wish to be represented for collective bargaining.

ADMINISTRATION OF THE WAGNER ACT

To administer this law, Congress created a new National Labor Relations Board composed of three members to be appointed by the President and confirmed by the Senate. The members served staggered terms of five years each.

Creation of the National Labor Relations Board to administer the Wagner Act was historically significant. For more than a hundred years, labor law in the United States had been fashioned by the courts, guided by ancient principles of the common law. The Wagner Act not only established a new code of rights for workers, but it entrusted the administration of those rights to a single federal agency, which, over the years, would establish a uniform, national body of precedents interpreting those rights in myriad situations. Although the federal courts of appeals and the Supreme Court were authorized to review the NLRB's unfair labor practice decisions, it was the Board that bore primary and continuing responsibility for making the new rights of American workers a reality.

Secretary of Labor Frances Perkins unsuccessfully argued that the NLRB should be part of the Labor Department, but Senator Wagner insisted that the Board be truly independent of the executive. The House Labor Committee stressed the "necessity of establishing a board with independence and dignity, in order to give it a national prestige adequate to the important functions conferred upon it."

Congress modeled the Labor Board on the Federal Trade Commission, one of the earliest of the quasi-judicial, independent federal agencies. The three-member NLRB was entrusted with administering both the unfair labor practice and the election provisions of the law. In Section 9, Congress spelled out the Board's authority to conduct elections, and in Section 10, Congress spelled out the Board's authority and procedures for determining whether an unfair labor practice had occurred.

The NLRB's authority on finding a violation was to issue a "cease and desist" order against the violator and to take other "affirmative action, including reinstatement of employees with or without back pay," in order to effectuate the statute's policies. The Wagner Act is a remedial statute—one designed to prevent and stop illegal conduct—rather than a criminal statute—one designed to punish law violators.

Congress gave the NLRB power to issue "complaints," to conduct hearings, to determine whether violations had occurred, and to issue orders to stop and remedy violations. But the Board's orders are not self-enforcing. The Board was, therefore, authorized to petition a federal court of appeals to enforce its decisions. (The complex relationship between the Board and the courts will be discussed in Chapter VI.)

The staff of the Wagner Act NLRB was divided between a headquarters staff in Washington and a field staff in regional offices throughout the country.

The Washington staff was headed by the three Presidentially appointed members. Under their supervision were the following major divisions: The Litigation Section, directed by the NLRB's general counsel, prosecuted unfair labor practice cases before the Board and represented it before the courts. The Review Section, also supervised by the NLRB general counsel, reviewed the transcripts of cases and drafted preliminary decisions for the Board's consideration. The Office of the Executive Secretary directed the internal administrative operations of the NLRB and the regional offices. The Economics Section performed a number of tasks, chief among which was preparation of research monographs on subjects relevant to the Board's work. The Information Section dealt with the press and prepared materials about the NLRB for the general public.

At the outset of its work in 1935, the Board established twenty-one regional offices in major urban centers. Each region was staffed by a regional director and a regional attorney, who supervised the work of attorneys and investigators.

In 1938, the Board established a Division of Trial Examiners that presided over unfair labor practice and representation hearings. This division was administratively separate from the remainder of the NLRB's staff because of the judicial character of the work of trial examiners.

EARLY YEARS OF THE NLRB

Selecting leadership for the new agency was not easy for the White House. As Roosevelt's Secretary of Labor, Frances Perkins, later wrote:

> It has always been hard to find just the right people willing to serve, for they must be judicial in temperament and yet have plenty of firmness. It is a grueling job. Board members are constantly exposed to condemnation for following what they believe to be the meaning of the law.

After many refusals, the President chose J. Warren Madden, dean of the University of Pittsburgh Law School, as the Board's first Chairman. Events of the decade proved that this was a superb choice, for Madden combined rare qualities of toughness, indefatigability, imagination, and compassion. Joining him as the agency's first members were Edwin S. Smith, who had served on the National Labor Relations Board created by Resolution 44 (described in Chapter I), and John M. Carmody, a member of the Railway Labor Act's National Mediation Board.

As its first general counsel, the Board selected Charles Fahy, a remarkable public servant, who has also served with distinction as solicitor general and thereafter as a judge of the court of appeals of the District of Columbia circuit. To this gentle, scholarly lawyer would fall the task of preparing for the inevitable attack on the statute's constitutionality.

On the day that President Roosevelt signed the Wagner Act, the National Association of Manufacturers issued a memorandum denouncing it as unconstitutional. Several weeks after that, the American Liberty League, an organization consisting of many of the country's largest employers, issued a 127-page broadside that argued against the constitutionality of the law and advised employers that the law could be disregarded. "We have no hesitancy," the Liberty League's lawyers said, "in considering [the Wagner Act] unconstitutional and that it constitutes a complete departure from constitutional and traditional theories of government."

Others joined in the assault. Conservative columnist Bernarr MacFadden exclaimed: "The Wagner labor law has industry by the throat."

There was good reason for employers to doubt the constitutionality of the Wagner Act, for the Supreme Court had consistently invalidated other major New Deal statutes on various grounds. With recent Supreme Court decisions as their guide, the lower federal courts issued nearly one hundred injunctions against the operation of the Wagner Act and the NLRB between 1935 and 1937. These injunctions effectively tied the Board's hands until the Supreme Court could rule on the Constitutional issues. In October, 1936, a writer in *The New Republic* commented: "The chief reason why there has been no news about the Board's achievements is that there have been no achievements. . . . The Board is . . . bordering on suspended animation."

The stage was being set for one of the crucial legal contests of the century. At stake was not only the survival of the Wagner Act but also other New Deal legislation and the credibility of Roosevelt's leadership. In 1935, the Supreme Court had invalidated the Railroad Retirement Act, the National Industrial Recovery Act, and the Farm Mortgage Act. In January, 1936, it struck down the Agricultural Adjustment Act. Later that year, it held unconstitutional the labor provisions of the Bituminous Coal Conservation Act, the Municipal Bankruptcy Act, and New York's minimum-wage law.

In November, 1936, President Roosevelt was re-elected by a landslide. He complained bitterly of the tyranny of the Supreme Court's "nine old men," who were destroying the statutory foundations of the New Deal. In February, 1937, several weeks after his second inauguration, he surprised the nation with a plan to appoint one new Supreme Court justice for each justice over age seventy, up to a maximum of six. This was his "court-packing plan," which overnight provoked a national controversy. During the spring of 1937, as the controversy brewed on Capitol Hill and across the country, the constitutionality of the Wagner Act reached the Supreme Court in five test cases.

By the narrowest of margins, five to four, the Supreme Court upheld the constitutionality of the Wagner Act on April 12, 1937. This victory for the New Deal, combined with growing public opposition to the court-packing plan, saved both the Supreme Court and the Wagner Act.

The five test cases involved different industries and diverse issues. They had been carefully selected and managed through the lower federal courts by NLRB General Counsel Fahy and his staff in order to present the strongest possible position to the high Court.

The most important of the five was the *Jones & Laughlin Steel Corporation* case. In this case, the NLRB had ruled that a number of employees had been discriminatorily discharged for their union activity in violation of the Act's Section 8(3).

The employer's response was that the Wagner Act was invalid on two grounds: first, that Jones & Laughlin, a manufacturer, did not "affect" interstate commerce within the meaning of the Constitution and, second, that the exclusive representation provisions of the Wagner Act violated the employer's "right to conduct its business in an orderly manner without being subject to arbitrary restraints."

The interstate commerce issue was the more difficult for the defenders of the Act, for as recently as 1936 the Supreme Court had taken a narrow view of Congress's power to regulate manufacturing under the commerce clause. In the *Jones & Laughlin* case, however, the Court made a pivotal shift in its thinking and sustained Congress's power to regulate manufacturing enterprises that *affect* interstate commerce, even though they are not *engaged* directly in commerce. The Court recalled the effects of the 1919 steel strike to illustrate how labor disputes in manufacturing industries can impede the flow of goods in interstate commerce, for during that strike there simply was no steel to ship in commerce.

Answering the contention that the Wagner Act unconstitutionally deprived the employer of freedom to conduct its business, the high Court said that employees "have as clear a right to organize and select their representatives for lawful purposes as the [employer] has to organize its business and select its own officers and agents." Perhaps the most famous passage from the Court's *Jones & Laughlin* opinion is this affirmation of the historical imperative of collective bargaining to promote industrial peace:

> Experience has abundantly demonstrated that the recognition of the right of employees to self-organization and to have representatives of their own choosing for the purpose of collective bargaining is often an essential condition of industrial peace. Refusal to confer and negotiate has been one of the most prolific causes of strife. This is such an outstanding fact in the history of labor disturbances that it is a proper subject of judicial notice and requires no citation of instances.

A contemporary periodical reported that a jubilant Pennsylvania steelworker proclaimed: "I mighty glad to hear Wagner Act went constitutional. Now Aliquippa become part of United States."

Within days after the *Jones & Laughlin* decision, the NLRB was inundated with thousands of new cases, which it was wholly unprepared to handle. The Board later reported that after the Constitutional decisions its case load rose at the rate of approximately 1,000 per cent. To help the Board meet this work load, Congress appropriated additional funds in August, 1937, but the young agency was still unable to meet its rising volume of cases.

Paradoxically, in the years immediately following the Constitutional cases, when the work of administering the Wagner Act truly began, the NLRB was buffeted by both internal and external problems.

Internally, many of the NLRB's problems surfaced with Roosevelt's appointment in 1939 of William Morris Leiserson, a distinguished professor of economics, an arbitrator, and a former member of the National Mediation Board. There is reason to believe that he was appointed by the White House with a mandate to reorganize the NLRB, so as to pacify the Board's AFL and management critics. Leiserson was sharply critical of the NLRB's executive secretary, Nathan Witt, and sought repeatedly to have him removed. He also differed frequently on policy matters with fellow Board member Edwin S. Smith. In essence, Smith was thought to lean favorably towards the new Congress of Industrial Organizations, while Leiserson tended towards the positions of the AFL. On a philosophical level, Leiserson was critical of what he perceived as the inordinate influence of lawyers and "legalism" in the Board's work.

In 1940, Chairman J. Warren Madden's term was to expire. John L. Lewis of the CIO urged the President to reappoint Madden, but the AFL and management opposed his reappointment. Responding to these pressures, Roosevelt declined to reappoint Madden and chose, instead, Harry A. Millis of the University of Chicago as the new Chairman. Millis and Leiserson saw things very much alike, and overnight they formed a majority within the Board in common opposition to Edwin S. Smith. In 1941, Smith's term expired, and Roosevelt appointed Gerard D. Reilly, a conservative lawyer and former solicitor of the Labor Department.

The NLRB's internal problems were worsened by a lack of continuity in the service of members. Not one member was reappointed for a full second term of five years. New members tended to reconsider prior Board policies and to reverse even recent precedents. Switches in policies and precedents made the Board highly vulnerable to criticism—some valid and some opportunistic—that the Board was unpredictable, unstable, and partisan. Such criticism has dogged the Board throughout its life. (See Chapter IX.)

Externally, the Board was the subject of virulent attacks from the management community, which charged it with a prolabor bias, and from the AFL, which charged it with a pro-CIO bias. These criticisms came to a head in 1939, during an ugly series of hearings conducted by Representative Howard Smith of Virginia, who charged the NLRB both with a lack of objectivity and with left-wing domination. The charges were not proven, nor were they susceptible to reliable proof. Students of the late 1930's believe that the NLRB, like other federal agencies, undoubtedly had its share of Communists, perhaps even a few in high places. The charges were, however, grossly inflated for partisan purposes, and their effect was to undermine the Board's morale and its public effectiveness. Because the Wagner Act was clearly designed to aid labor, it is hardly surprising that the NLRB and its staff were sympathetic to the labor movement, sometimes with an excess of zeal over judgment. An article in *Fortune* in 1938, entitled "The G——— D——— Labor Board," summed up the emotionally charged atmosphere in which the Board worked:

. . . industrial relations have achieved the unreasoning bitterness of a holy war. They have become a battlefield of slogans and shibboleths, of coercion and propaganda, of intimidation and mutual accusation, of guerrilla warfare and strikes. It is this battlefield that the NLRB has invaded—intending, according to its sponsors, to "smooth out obstructions to the free flow of commerce"—succeeding, according to its opponents, in making an already intolerable situation infinitely worse. Drawn up on one side is an almost solid phalanx of U.S. industry led by the National Association of Manufacturers and the U.S. Chamber of Commerce, and at the moment heavily supported by the leaders of the AF of L. On the other side is the CIO and what is probably a majority of the rank and file of *organized* labor.

Despite these internal and external problems, the NLRB created by the Wagner Act performed minor miracles during its twelve years. It processed more than 100,000 unfair labor practice and representation cases. It defined basic statutory procedures for case handling. It enjoyed remarkable success in having its decisions sustained in the courts. And, ever so gradually, it began to build a solid body of labor jurisprudence —consisting of hundreds of reasoned decisions—giving specificity to the broad policies of the Wagner Act in an ever-changing panorama of individual situations.

Labor Relations Between 1935 and 1947

In 1935, as the Wagner Act and the NLRB were brought to life by Congress, the American labor movement entered a period of deep internal conflict. The source of this conflict was the disagreement over whether the AFL would pledge itself to engage in industrial unionism—the organization of the millions of hitherto unorganized workers in the mass production industries in units broadly inclusive of skilled and unskilled workers.

Since the 1890's, the AFL had emphasized craft unionism,

largely ignoring unskilled workers, who were by far the majority of the working population. Within the AFL, militant industrial unionists led by John L. Lewis of the United Mine Workers, Sidney Hillman of the Clothing Workers, David Dubinsky of the Ladies Garment Workers, and Charles Howard of the International Typographical Union—sought to persuade the AFL to seize the unique opportunity presented by the New Deal to organize mass production industries. At an historic convention of the AFL in Atlantic City late in 1935, tensions between craft and industrial unionists led to a rupture in the AFL. The industrial union leaders formed a Committee for Industrial Organization (CIO) in 1936 to attempt the task that the AFL shunned. Although they sought to work within the AFL, interpersonal relations between the AFL and CIO leaders became so strained that in August, 1936, the AFL expelled the ten national unions that had started the CIO.

The CIO then embarked upon the most ambitious and singularly successful organizing drive in American history. Led by Philip Murray, a vice-president of the United Mine Workers, the CIO's Steel Workers Organizing Committee attacked the basic steel industry with four hundred organizers. U.S. Steel Corporation, the industry's giant, quietly agreed to recognize the steelworkers' union in March, 1937, without a fight, a stunning victory for the new CIO. After a brief but highly successful strike at the Jones & Laughlin steel company the other leaders in this industry, called "Little Steel," fought back. A long and violent strike followed, highlighted by the tragic Memorial Day Massacre in Chicago on May 30, 1937; but the strike against "Little Steel" failed.

In the auto, textile, rubber, electrical parts, glass, clothing, and other industries, the CIO was on the move, calling strikes and sweeping in new members by the tens of thousands. By the end of 1937, the CIO claimed a membership of more than 3.5 million.

Public sympathy was largely with the CIO but cooled somewhat early in 1937, when the group adopted a new tactic, the sit-down strike. The best-known sit-down strike was called by the United Auto Workers (UAW) at a General Motors plant in Flint, Michigan. When General Motors refused to recognize the UAW, workers sat down at their machines and barricaded themselves inside. General Motors cut off the heat, but friends of the strikers smuggled in food and blankets. Local police tried to oust the strikers by force, but the strikers drove them off with bottles and metal parts. When the police used tear gas, the strikers replied with a fire hose. With the help of Michigan Governor Frank Murphy and a push from the White House, a settlement was negotiated in which General Motors recognized the union—another victory for the CIO in the auto industry.

The CIO grew. Its president, John L. Lewis, loomed over the late 1930's as an epic figure. Although the AFL's initial response had been to ignore the CIO, the success of industrial unionism jolted the AFL into action. Now large AFL unions—especially the Machinists, Electrical Workers, Carpenters, and Teamsters—entered the field to organize industrial workers in competition with the CIO.

For the new NLRB, the consequences of the AFL and CIO struggle were momentous. This internecine fight became a legal struggle over bargaining units and representation rights, bringing the battle between the AFL and the CIO to the doorstep of the NLRB. Although the new Board had fully expected to perform its work in an atmosphere of management hostility, it could not have expected to find itself in the middle of a labor civil war at the same time. This struggle, as already noted, led to sharp attacks on members of the Board and its staff, who were accused of bias in favor of the CIO, leading to the ouster of Chairman Madden and member Edwin S. Smith, as well as a number of staff members.

As the CIO sought to organize the mass production industries, some employers responded with traditional nineteenth-century antilabor tactics without regard to the rules of

fairness laid down by the Wagner Act. Many decisions of the
NLRB in the 1930's reflected management hostility to worker
organization and the CIO. As an outgrowth of the "Little
Steel" strike of 1937, for example, the Board found that the
giant Republic Steel Corporation had engaged in these unfair
labor practices:

> . . . espionage, shadowing, and beatings of organizers . . .
> announcements . . . that it would not sign any contract with
> the Union; . . . threats to discharge union members and to
> close its plants before recognizing the Union, and . . . other
> threats and warnings to employees regarding the Union; . . .
> attempts to turn civil authorities, business, and other interests
> against the Union in order to further its own anti-Union activi-
> ties; . . . incitement to violence and hysteria, in order to
> terrorize union adherents; . . . donation of tear and vomiting
> gas to the City of Massilon; . . . lay-offs, discharges, and
> lock-out.

During 1936 and 1937, the La Follette Civil Liberties Committee of the Senate conducted a series of hearings on employer tactics that revealed the use of uniformed police,
stockpiling of "industrial munitions," industrial espionage, and
the use of professional strikebreakers. Most of the committee's
findings involved activities that violated the Wagner Act, but
during this period the Board was paralyzed by injunctions
against its operation. Exposure of these tactics by the La Follette committee and unfair labor practice findings of the
NLRB aroused revulsion in the public mind and in the
management community itself. By the end of the 1930's, most
employers had abandoned these primitive forms of opposition
to unions.

As the 1930's drew to a close, the economy had become
revitalized, and unemployment dropped. The worst of the
Great Depression was over. But what lay ahead—visible and
menacing in Western Europe and the Far East—was global
warfare.

When America entered World War II in December, 1941,

demands of defense production created a scarcity of labor. Throughout the war, labor cooperated with the government's pleas for uninterrupted production and a moratorium on strikes. Most of labor submitted to wage-price controls. (John L. Lewis and his United Mine Workers were an exception. Lewis had given up the CIO presidency in November, 1940, when the labor movement refused to follow his endorsement of Wendell Willkie against President Roosevelt's third-term bid.) The War Labor Board settled disputes by the thousands.

When the war ended, labor was restless. It feared that massive unemployment would immediately return and that the end of defense production would bring a return to depression. Although there was much talk of and some planning for reconversion to peacetime production, no one knew whether or how the economy could accommodate the 12 million men and women in the armed forces, as well as the 8 million in defense industries.

In the three months between V–E and V–J days in 1945, unemployment increased from 500,000 to 1 million. And, after the surrender of Japan, defense contracts in the amount of $20 billion were abruptly canceled, and unemployment increased once more—this time to 3 million workers.

To labor's fears of mass unemployment was added the further fear of inflation and reduced earnings. Wartime wage-price controls were scheduled to expire in June, 1946. President Harry S. Truman sought an extension, but Congress was unresponsive. Prices rose dramatically, as consumer demand for goods and services was unleashed.

Convinced that it had made greater sacrifices during the war than management, labor made a desperate effort to catch up. The mass production industries had been organized only shortly before the war; and collective bargaining had been frozen almost immediately thereafter by wartime controls. Labor thus sought to make up for years of waiting. What followed was a wave of strikes in basic industries in late 1945 and all of 1946. For war-weary, crisis-weary Americans who wished to return to the mythical state of "normalcy," the first year after World War II was one of persistent labor strife.

In November, 1945, the United Auto Workers called a strike against General Motors involving 180,000 workers for 113 days. In the spring of 1946, a soft-coal industry strike caused industrial users and homeowners great inconvenience. No sooner had this strike been settled than John L. Lewis and his union threatened another nationwide strike.

In May, 1946, despite Presidential seizure, 300,000 railroad workers struck the nation's railroads. This was settled two days later, while President Truman was asking a joint session of Congress for authority to draft strikers into the army.

The strike statistics for 1946 were staggering: There had been 5,000 strikes, involving 4,600,000 workers, with a loss of 107,475,000 man-days of work. In February, 1946, more man-days were lost through strikes than in 1943 and 1944 combined.

Moreover, the years after the war witnessed a paranoid fear of domestic subversion. The CIO began to face up to its long-term problem of Communist leadership. It has been estimated that, in 1946, unions with Communist leadership controlled 15 per cent of the CIO's membership. Some feared that Communist-led unions would become Soviet Russia's fifth column in America.

Congress, in 1946, was responsive to the public temper. It passed a modest series of revisions to the Wagner Act, which President Truman vetoed. Labor legislation was a common subject in Congress during 1946. It seemed all but inevitable that changes in the Wagner Act lay ahead.

In the November, 1946, congressional elections, the Republican campaign slogan was simply: "Had enough?" Labor problems were not the only subject in the minds of voters when they elected a Republican Congress—the first since 1930—in those elections. But the new congressional leadership had been elected over labor's opposition and in response to public sentiment against "labor's excesses"—a phrase commonly used in

1946 and 1947. The Eightieth Congress would "put labor in its place."

The year 1947 was to be crucial. Franklin D. Roosevelt was dead; the Depression had blended into the horror of world war; the new peace was uneasy; John L. Lewis had receded into a bitter isolation from the labor movement; an accidental President, Harry S. Truman, was being tested by a Congress controlled by Republicans; and the public no longer saw labor as the underdog but as an economic and political threat to postwar society.

III

The Taft-Hartley Act

Paul Herzog, the brilliant young Chairman of the NLRB, appointed in 1945, contended before the House and Senate Labor committees in 1947 that the Wagner Act had never operated in normal times: During its first six years, 1935–41, the nation was in the grip of the Depression; the system of elections and collective bargaining established by the Act was still new; and the labor movement was undergoing structural change and intense internal warfare. During the second 6-year period, 1941–47, America was at war or engaged in post-war reconversion; the economy was under wage and price controls; collective bargaining had been largely suspended during the control period; and the immediate postwar period was economically atypical. Implicit in Herzog's testimony was the suggestion that Congress should approach the task of revising the Wagner Act carefully and moderately. But Congress was not in a mood for moderation, nor was the nation. Weary from the gloom of the Depression and the trauma of war, fearful of an uncertain future, American public opinion was aroused to change national labor policy.

LEGISLATIVE HISTORY OF THE TAFT-HARTLEY ACT

In 1947, Harry Truman sat uneasily in the White House. And in the Senate of the new Eightieth Congress, the undisputed leader of the Republican majority was Robert A. Taft, a high-minded conservative from Ohio. Truman and Taft were the protagonists in the supercharged legislative drama over the Taft-Hartley Act.

From the moment the Wagner Act had become law, large segments of the business community had sought to repeal it or to amend it in ways acceptable to employers. Leading the fight for amendments to the Wagner Act were the National Association of Manufacturers and the U.S. Chamber of Commerce, both of which made revision of the Wagner Act a top legislative priority. Senator George D. Aiken of Vermont charged on the floor of the Senate in May, 1947, that the National Association of Manufacturers alone had spent no less than $100 million in a campaign to revise the Wagner Act.

Ostensibly, the goal of the business community was to make the law more equitable and, in particular, to cure its one-sided application to management of unfair labor practice restrictions. In reality, its more significant purpose was to curb the growing economic and political power of organized labor. The legislative debate over the merits of revision in the law masked a classic confrontation—a power struggle—between the business community and the labor movement. The partisans on each side were bitter and determined. The emotional heat of such an atmosphere was poorly suited to a rational, balanced review of the 12-year record of the Wagner Act and the NLRB. It was rather a political-economic showdown. The business community won decisively but not easily.

When the Eightieth Congress organized itself in January, 1947, Senator Taft became chairman of the Senate Labor Committee. His counterpart in the House of Representatives was a little-known congressman from New Jersey, Fred A. Hartley, Jr., who was chairman of the House Committee on Education and Labor. Taft was both a leader of his party and perhaps the best-known Republican in the country; he aspired to his party's Presidential nomination in 1948 and was favored by many of his congressional colleagues. His brilliant legal mind and unquestioned integrity made him a figure of great

respect, although some found him a rather colorless and hu-
morless public personality.

By contrast, Representative Hartley was both little known
and little respected. His predecessor as chairman of the House
Education and Labor Committee charged—and Hartley did
not deny—that during his ten years' service on the committee
he had attended only six meetings. (An interesting sidelight
is that at the time of Hartley's chairmanship the membership
of the House Labor Committee included two young freshmen
congressmen: John F. Kennedy from Massachusetts and
Richard M. Nixon from California.)

Both the Senate and House committees held hearings on
the numerous labor bills that were introduced in the early
days of the Eightieth Congress. Scholars give the Senate Labor
Committee under Taft's chairmanship high marks for fairness,
while almost uniformly they give low marks to Hartley's
House committee for a lack of fairness and objectivity.

The Senate committee conducted lengthy hearings, listening
to public, labor, and management witnesses whose testimony
ultimately was published in four bound volumes. The bill that
the Senate committee finally reported, S. 1126, was a complex
68-page document. When it reached the Senate floor,
the ensuing debate was entirely predictable. Republicans and
conservative Democrats defended the Taft bill as essential
to achieve fairness and evenhandedness in the Wagner Act.
Its complex provisions were carefully reviewed and fully debated. Northern Democrats attacked the bill as punitive, ill-
conceived, unnecessary, and calculated to undermine the
rights of workers. The political-ideological lines were drawn,
and the outcome was never seriously in doubt. On May 13,
1947, after nine days of floor debate, the Senate approved the
Taft bill by a vote of sixty-eight to twenty-four.

The story in the House was very different. Hearings in the
House committee were much shorter. Despite the fact that
more than half of the testimony was expressly critical of the
NLRB's performance, the Board was granted only three hours

to respond—less than had been granted to several individual critics. More serious, however, was sharp and repeated criticism that majority members of the committee operated in a clandestine fashion to deprive minority members of an opportunity to participate in drafting the committee bill.

Committee hearings, for example, ended in the House on March 15. According to angry minority Democrats in their minority report, on April 10 the Hartley bill, H.R. 3020, was introduced on the floor, and on the same day, they were shown a copy of it for the first time. They were then told that their minority report had to be prepared within two days. This procedure, the minority charged, not only cut them out of the deliberative work of the committee but was also an unaccustomed breach of legislative ethics.

Moreover, a major controversy emerged over the authorship of the Hartley bill. While the evidence is still not clear, there seems little doubt that it was primarily drafted by a cadre of management lawyers, chiefly Gerald Morgan, a prominent corporation lawyer. Morgan testified before a congressional committee in 1949 that he was the main author of the House committee bill and that he had been assisted by two other management lawyers. He admitted further that he received a fee of $7,500 from the Republican National Committee for his drafting work. The minority proclaimed bitterly on the floor of the House that the committee bill had been written by the National Association of Manufacturers, and recent scholarship shows that the Hartley bill, if not written by the association, bore remarkable similarities to one that it had proposed.

Debate on the House committee bill began on the House floor on April 15, under a rule that limited debate to six hours. Again, the minority bitterly charged that the bill was too complex to be debated in this allotted time, particularly because some members had not even had time to read the committee's reports. Nonetheless, the debate ended in a vote on April 17, 308 to 107 in favor of the committee bill.

Although the House and Senate bills had many features in common, the House bill was far more punitive and restrictive from labor's point of view. Because of the differences between the bills, it was necessary to convene a conference committee. Representative Hartley later wrote that his strategy in the House Labor Committee was to write the toughest bill he could, so that in conference the Taft bill would seem moderate and reasonable by comparison; therefore, it would ultimately be easier to secure approval of the Taft bill. Whether this was, indeed, a calculated strategy or simply a clever afterthought on Hartley's part has been a subject of unresolved discussion ever since.

In any event, the conferees did, in fact, agree on a compromise bill that followed the main outlines of the Taft bill and rejected the harshest features of the Hartley legislation. The conference committee performed its work with acute awareness of the possibility that a particularly tough bill might be vetoed by the President. Thus, the committee's strategy was to fashion a bill that might escape a veto or that, even if vetoed, would have sufficient support in both chambers to override a veto.

After two weeks, the conference committee settled on a compromise bill, the main features of which would:

1. Increase the size of the NLRB from three to five members.
2. Require that the Board's findings of fact be supported by "substantial evidence" on the whole record, not on a piecemeal basis.
3. Create an independent NLRB general counsel to serve as the Board's prosecuting arm, to replace the general counsel who had functioned as a part of the Board.
4. Outlaw the closed shop and limit the union shop to instances in which employees had approved it by a majority, secret-ballot vote.
5. Permit the states to prohibit union shop contracts and other compulsory membership clauses.

6. Prohibit union interference with Section 7 rights of employees and at the same time amend Section 7 itself to protect the right of employees to "refrain" from engaging in union activities.
7. Prohibit unions from causing employers to discriminate against employees.
8. Require unions to bargain in good faith.
9. Prohibit unions from engaging in secondary boycotts and jurisdictional disputes.
10. Prohibit "featherbedding."
11. Prohibit unions from charging excessive dues and initiation fees.
12. Require unions and employers to give notice before terminating a contract or striking.
13. Define the obligation to bargain more specifically.
14. Protect employer "free speech."
15. Exclude workers in nonprofit hospitals and supervisors from the coverage of the law.
16. Create a new Federal Mediation and Conciliation Service.
17. Authorize the President to invoke procedures leading to an 80-day national emergency dispute injunction.
18. Make unions suable in the federal courts in their own name and permit suits to enforce collective bargaining agreements.
19. Prohibit check-off arrangements (deduction of union dues and fees), except under strict conditions.
20. Require union officials to execute non-Communist affidavits as the price of protection of the law.
21. Prohibit union contributions to federal election campaigns.
22. Prohibit federal employee strikes.
23. Permit employees to petition to decertify a bargaining agent and permit employers to file election petitions.
24. Require the NLRB to seek injunctions against unions believed to have engaged in secondary boycotts or jurisdictional strikes.

25. Create a joint congressional committee to study the operation of the new law.

On June 4, the House approved the conference bill by a vote of 320–79 after a debate of one hour. The Senate passed the bill by 57–17 on June 6. On June 9, the bill was sent to the White House.

The pressure that had been on Congress during the Taft-Hartley debates now was directed at the White House. Business and most farm groups wrote and telegraphed the President to sign the bill, while labor and liberal groups urged a veto. Rallies of union members were held throughout the country to denounce Taft-Hartley as a "slave labor bill." Proponents and opponents spent huge sums for radio and newspaper advertisements.

Within the White House, President Truman's Cabinet and staff advisers were divided over the course he should follow. In favor of signing the bill were its probable passage over a Presidential veto, public opinion generally favoring the bill, and the disadvantage, in the 1948 elections, of having tried to block a bill that the public apparently supported. In favor of a veto were the Democratic Party's close ties to labor, the President's need for labor support in 1948, and the opposition to the bill from the liberal wing of the Democratic Party.

On June 20, President Truman sent a veto message to Congress. It was a strong message, which, according to the *New York Times,* used twenty-four adjectives, such as "dangerous," "unworkable," "harsh," "arbitrary," and "drastic," to attack the Taft-Hartley bill. That same evening, he addressed the nation on radio and explained his reasons. Senator Taft followed in a separate radio address defending the bill.

The same day the House overrode the veto within an hour after receiving the President's message. Three days later the Senate, too, overrode the veto by a wide margin. The Taft-Hartley Act became effective on August 22, 1947.

Major Policies of the Taft-Hartley Act

In a sense, the Taft-Hartley Act is several laws, for it deals with a number of separate kinds of labor problems, many unrelated to the work of the NLRB. It is also a highly complex law whose meaning is still being explored by the NLRB and the courts year by year. To understand the scope of Taft-Hartley as it applies to the National Labor Relations Board, it is useful to examine three major categories of changes that it made: changes affecting the structure of the Board and its administration; changes in the unfair labor practice provisions of the law; and changes in the representation election provisions of the law.

Changes in the Structure of the Board

Taft-Hartley expanded the Board from three to five members and authorized it to sit in panels of three members to exercise its various powers. Given the Board's heavy work load, this was not a controversial amendment.

The most important change in the Board made by Taft-Hartley was the creation of the office of an independent NLRB general counsel to be appointed by the President. He would act as a prosecutor under the Act and supervise all of the Board's attorneys, except for the Board's own legal advisers and the legal advisers attached to individual Board members. The theory of establishing an independent prosecutor within the agency was that the Board should function like a court and be totally divorced from the prosecutory function.

Management critics of the Board had charged for twelve years that the Board acted as prosecutor and judge. By this, they meant that, under the Wagner Act, the Board authorized the issuance of complaints against employers and that, following a hearing and a trial examiner's decision, the Board would review the evidence to determine whether the employer had committed an unfair labor practice. This criticism had little merit, because the NLRB created internal separations between its prosecutory and adjudicative work. Moreover, *all* other federal regulatory agencies combined these functions in the interest of consistent administration of their statutes. They, like the NLRB, internally separated their functions, as, indeed, they were required to do by the Administrative Procedure Act. Nonetheless, Congress treated the NLRB differently from all other agencies by giving its general counsel final authority to issue complaints. Within a year after the law's passage, the Board and its newly independent general counsel became entangled in a nasty fight over the administration and interpretation of the law. (The facts and implications of that conflict will be discussed later in this chapter.)

Another major change that Taft-Hartley effected was to prohibit the Board from employing attorneys to review records of hearings and to draft opinions for the Board, except for attorneys on the staffs of individual Board members. The point of this amendment was simply to require the Board to abolish its old review section, which was composed of lawyers who performed background staff work on pending cases for the entire NLRB. It had come under criticism from the management community, which charged that it had a prolabor bias and that its work deprived individual Board members of the practical ability to shape and influence the outcome of cases. In eliminating the review section, Congress provided that each member of the Board would employ a personal staff of attorneys to perform such staff work for him as an individual.

Congress also forbade the NLRB to employ anyone to engage in the work of "economic analysis." In the early years of the Wagner Act, the Board established a Division of Economic Research to assist it in understanding labor-relations trends in relation to its work. This division came in sharp conflict with the NLRB's general counsel in the late 1930's over its director's political views, and, more importantly, it came under fire by the Smith committee in 1939 (see Chapter II). Congress attached a rider to the Board's appropriation bill in 1940, eliminating the work of this division, so that as a practical matter, Taft-Hartley merely reaffirmed Congress's earlier decision to require the Board to eliminate the Economic Research Division.

Many scholars believe that this limitation on the Board's authority to engage in economic research was short-sighted. Lacking such resources, the Board has been required to formulate significant policies without the guidance of economic data as to the probable impact on the parties. Most other federal regulatory agencies regard economic research as among their most important tools in implementing congressional policy. But Congress, for reasons that can only be explained by peculiar historical circumstances of the late 1930's, directed the NLRB to perform its sensitive work in the labor-relations field without the benefit of an economic research component.

Changes in the Law of Unfair Labor Practices

Responding to management's claim that the Wagner Act was lopsided in its regulation only of *employer* unfair labor practices, and based on testimony of improper conduct by unions, Congress defined six union unfair labor practices in Taft-Hartley.

Section 8(b) (1) prohibits unions from interfering with the rights of employees defined in Section 7 of the original Act. One of the principal purposes of this provision has been to enable the NLRB to deal with union violence against employees. This unfair practice section of the law also prohibits union interference with the right of management to select its own representatives for purposes of collective bargaining, although this prohibition has seldom been the subject of serious attention.

Section 8(b) (2) makes it unlawful for a union to cause an employer to discriminate against an employee in violation of Section 8(a) (3). This prohibition, which must be read in conjunction with amended Section 8(a) (3), does several things: First, it declares that the closed shop is illegal, and it authorizes a union shop agreement with an employer only if employees are given a grace period of thirty days after their hire (or after the execution of a union shop contract) before they can be required to join a union. Second, it provides that unions and employers cannot interfere with an employee's job rights —even under a union shop contract—except if the employee fails to pay uniform, periodic dues and initiation fees. This means, for example, that a union cannot fine a member for failing to attend a union meeting and threaten to get him fired unless he pays the fine, for the law now states that a union can require a member to pay nothing but dues and initiation fees in order to hold his job. Third, Section 8(b) (2) provides that unions cannot put pressure on employers to engage in discrimination against employees, either to encourage or discourage union membership. This prohibition means, for example, that a union cannot ask an employer to discharge an employee who has complained about the union and who seeks to have it replaced with another union.

Section 8(b) (3) imposes on unions the same obligation to bargain in good faith that the Wagner Act imposed on employers. Although there had been no pervasive problem with unions refusing to bargain in good faith, some unions had presented employers with a printed contract and demanded that the employers "take it or leave it" without discussion or good faith bargaining.

Section 8(b) (4), by far the most complex provision of the Taft-Hartley Act, is known as the secondary boycott prohibition. For many years, the courts had attempted to define a secondary boycott and to impose judicially promulgated limitations on its use. In essence, Congress declared that it is unfair for a union that has a primary dispute with one employer to put pressure on a second employer to cause him to stop doing business with the first employer. Congress sought to achieve this objective by drawing a circle around the primary dispute and prohibiting a union from extending that dispute to neutral employers and employees. This section also prohibited strikes or threats in aid of jurisdictional disputes between unions over the right to perform particular work. Section 8(b) (4) has been the source of endless litigation and overwhelming confusion. In 1959, Congress again tried to make the law of secondary boycott clear and precise.

Section 8(b) (5) prohibits unions from charging excessive dues or initiation fees. The basis for this prohibition was evidence that a few unions charged exorbitant dues and initiation fees as a device for excluding workers from their industries. This practice was limited to a few craft unions that sought to keep their wages high by creating an artificial labor scarcity.

Section 8(b) (6), the final union unfair labor practice regulation, was designed to deal with the problem of "featherbedding"—requiring employers to pay employees for services not performed. Congress was very much concerned about featherbedding practices in 1947, and in the previous year, it enacted a criminal statute specifically to prohibit such practices in the broadcast industry. Because the constitutionality of the criminal statute was being tested during the Taft-Hartley debates, however, Congress approached the problem very gingerly in Section 8(b) (6). Within a few years, judicial decisions made it clear that this section is, in practice, virtually meaningless, because it contains an enormous loophole that permits unions to negotiate contracts providing that employees may be paid for useless and unneeded work. This section only prohibits causing an employer to pay for the performance of no work whatever.

Related to the six new union unfair labor practices were two other important provisions, Sections 8(c) and (d). Section 8(c) is commonly known as the "free speech clause." In substance, it provides that the expression of views, arguments, or opinion "shall not . . . be evidence of an unfair labor practice . . . if such expression contains no threat of reprisal or force or promise of benefit." The genesis of this provision was the charge by employers that the NLRB during the Wagner Act years "muzzled" employers, interfering with their First Amendment rights of free expression. Although the Supreme Court had held in the mid-1940's that employers were entitled to express their opinions on labor-relations issues to employees, Congress evidently believed that it was necessary to make clear that the NLRB could not circumscribe free speech under the guise of an unfair labor practice. Consistent with the Supreme Court's rulings, however, Congress provided in Section 8(c) that "free speech" does not permit employers or unions to threaten employees, to use force against them, or to make promises of benefit, in violation of other sections of the Act. The Board's interpretation of Section 8(c) has always been controversial: Employers usually charge that the Board applies it too narrowly; unions charge that the Board applies it too generously.

In Section 8(d), Congress spelled out the meaning of the duty to bargain in good faith. This section reflects the Board's own decisions during the Wagner Act years. It states:

> To bargain collectively is the performance of the mutual obligation of the employer and the representative of the employees to meet at reasonable times and confer in good faith with respect to wages, hours and other terms and conditions of employment . . . and the execution of a written contract incorporating any agreement reached if requested by either party, but such obligation does not compel either party to agree to a proposal or require the making of a concession.

Additionally, Section 8(d) requires parties to give each other and the Federal Mediation and Conciliation Service notice of their desire to terminate or modify an existing collective agreement. This portion of Section 8(d), which has complex ramifications, was designed to prevent abrupt termination of contracts and sudden strikes. It requires that the parties will engage in collective bargaining without strikes or lockouts for no less than sixty days before termination of a contract, and it affords mediation agencies an opportunity to intervene in labor disputes to help effectuate a peaceful settlement.

Changes in the Law of Representation Proceedings

Taft-Hartley left the structure and basic principles of representation elections intact but made several significant additions. These changes are contained primarily in amendments to Sections 2 and 9 of the Wagner Act.

One prominent change is the exclusion of supervisors from bargaining units. This change was prompted by management's arguments that supervisors ought to owe their loyalty solely to management. If supervisors belong to rank-and-file unions, management contended, whom can management rely upon to assure that its interests are adequately safeguarded? Despite great controversy, Congress accepted this argument and excluded supervisors from coverage of the Act.

Congress also directed the Board to grant special treatment to three other classes of employees: professional employees, craftsmen, and plant guards. Each of these classes of employees had had a unique history under the Wagner Act. In summary, professional employees are not to be included in a bargaining unit with nonprofessional employees, unless a majority of the professionals vote for inclusion. Craftsmen were given a special status: Congress said the Board could not rule that a bargaining unit of craftsmen was not appropriate solely on the ground that a different unit had been established by a prior unit determination, unless a majority of the craftsmen voted against separate representation. And plant guards, because of their special security functions, were not to be included in a bargaining unit with other employees.

Congress added four new kinds of elections, supplementing the Wagner Act election to certify a bargaining agent:

1. *Elections on employer petitions.* This is like the Wagner Act representation election, except that it can be initiated by an employer. Under the Wagner Act only a union or employees could file an election petition, and, except in unusual circumstances, employers could not. Now an employer who is faced with a union's demand for recognition may ask the Board to conduct an election.

2. *Decertification election petitions.* Congress established an election procedure for employees to oust a union as their bargaining agent.

3. *Union security elections.* In order to negotiate a union shop agreement, the parties were now required to have the prior approval of employees, as expressed in a secret-ballot election conducted by the NLRB. Within four years, Congress repealed this union shop authorization election provision, because unions almost invariably won such elections. Hence, Congress concluded that it was a waste of time and money for the NLRB to conduct them.

4. *Union security de-authorization elections.* In addition to requiring a secret-ballot election of employees to authorize unions and employers to enter into union shop contracts, Congress created a de-authorization election proceeding by which employees could withdraw their approval from a union shop contract. When Congress repealed the union shop election authorization provisions, it left the de-authorization provisions. In the history of Taft-Hartley, the NLRB has been called upon to conduct relatively few de-authorization elections.

In three paragraphs of Section 9, Congress introduced indirect regulation of internal union affairs for the first time. Congress said, in effect, that, in order for unions to enjoy the coverage and protection of the Labor Act, they had to meet two broad requirements: First, they had to file detailed financial data and a variety of other data about themselves on official forms with the Secretary of Labor each year. Second, their officers had to file non-Communist affidavits, swearing that they were not members of the Communist Party or any other organization that believes in or teaches the overthrow of the government by violent or unconstitutional means. The non-Communist affidavit requirement stirred a storm of controversy and an endless succession of litigation over its exact meaning and constitutionality. In 1959, when Congress enacted the Landrum-Griffin Act, these requirements were repealed but were redefined in much more detailed form in that law. From the perspective of the 1970's, the non-Communist affidavit requirement seems rather quaint, but it was established by Congress at a time when the fear of Communists in the labor movement was at its apex.

There were, to be sure, many other detailed and technical ways in which the Taft-Hartley Act changed the substance and structure of the Wagner Act. But those reviewed above are of greatest historical and practical importance.

THE FIRST DECADE OF TAFT-HARTLEY

Labor was far from reconciled to Taft-Hartley as a permanent reality. Literally from the moment of the law's enactment, labor planned for its repeal.

The Campaign to Repeal Taft-Hartley

The year 1948 was a national election year, and the platform of the Democratic Party pledged repeal of Taft-Hartley. President Truman condemned the law and made repeal a major issue in his bid for election against Governor Thomas E. Dewey of New York, while Dewey ignored Taft-Hartley and conducted his campaign aloof from labor-management controversy.

Truman began his campaign before a hundred thousand supporters on Labor Day, 1948, in Detroit, attacking Taft-Hartley as a "dangerous weapon" placed in the hands of giant corporations by a Republican Congress. In the next two months, Truman traveled 31,700 miles, delivered 356 speeches, and everywhere repeated the theme that "the Republicans pushed through the Taft-Hartley law, which converted the National Labor Relations Board into an agency to hamstring union labor."

Congressman Hartley had just published a book that praised Taft-Hartley and implied that even stronger legislation was needed in the years ahead to curb union power. Truman quoted liberally from Hartley's book and warned that, if Dewey were elected, labor could anticipate that Republicans would "take the gloves off, and give you the bare knuckles."

Truman's victory over Dewey in November, 1948, was doubtless the greatest political upset of the twentieth century. Organized labor rejoiced—prematurely.

A confident President Truman advocated repeal of Taft-Hartley in his 1949 State of the Union message to Congress. It was a Democratic-controlled Congress; both Truman and the labor movement were optimistic.

Early in the Eighty-first Congress, Truman sought to redeem his campaign pledges for repeal. The chosen instrument was to be the Thomas-Lesinski bill. In substance, it would have repealed Taft-Hartley entirely and re-enacted the original Wagner Act. Later, in a so-called "second package," it would have proposed modest amendments to deal with secondary boycotts, jurisdictional disputes, and strikes over contract grievances.

Hearings on Thomas-Lesinski were conducted in the early months of 1949, and it was reported to the floors of both houses. The opponents of repeal—again a coalition of Republicans and Southern Democrats—devised their own strategies to block repeal. In the House, their strategy was to offer a substitute, the Wood bill, which would have made minor modifications in Taft-Hartley but substantially re-enacted it. In the Senate, their strategy was to amend Thomas-Lesinski to death, making it unacceptable to its supporters.

In the House, the opponents of Taft-Hartley were unable

to pass Thomas-Lesinski. Their sole accomplishment was to have the Wood bill recommitted to committee. And in the Senate, under Senator Taft's leadership, the supporters of Taft-Hartley succeeded in having their amendments to the Thomas-Lesinski bill adopted by a narrow margin. The Senate bill was then sent to the House of Representatives where it disappeared in committee and never reappeared.

These skirmishes in 1949 ended labor's campaign to repeal Taft-Hartley as a practical matter, even though Truman and labor would continue to give lip service to the need for repeal. Scholars have devoted considerable attention to the repeal movement and the reasons for its failure, concluding that the major flaw in labor's strategy was that it was rigidly uncompromising. Rather than acknowledging that some portions of Taft-Hartley were acceptable and concentrating on repeal of its most offensive provisions, labor demanded total repeal. It would not even consider amendments to the original Wagner Act until Taft-Hartley had been legislatively erased, but there were not enough votes to be found in the Congress for this rigid approach.

Labor argued that Truman had a mandate to secure repeal of Taft-Hartley, a plausible interpretation of his surprising victory in 1948. But Congress evidently did not believe that it had such a mandate, too.

In the twelve years following the enactment of Taft-Hartley, labor's legislative support was never sufficient to make another significant assault on it. On the other hand, supporters of more drastic labor legislation were similarly frustrated. The result was a legislative standoff. The labor drive for repeal, however, had another clearly seen result. As the veteran labor reporter A. H. Raskin put it: "One thing Taft-Hartley did accomplish. It got unions into politics on a year-round basis." From 1947 on, organized labor became permanently concerned with national political life.

The single change made in the Taft-Hartley Act during its first decade was noncontroversial. Taft-Hartley required the

Board to conduct elections to authorize unions to enter into union shop contracts with employers. Between 1947 and 1951, unions won these authorization elections in 97 per cent of all cases, usually by overwhelming majorities. This gave union bargainers a big push in seeking such contracts—and healthy wage boosts. Some 4,700 of these elections were conducted in 1948, when the CIO followed a policy of refusing to execute non-Communist affidavits required by Taft-Hartley. In a major decision, the Supreme Court invalidated these elections. To conduct them again—with wholly predictable results— would have cost the government more than $3 million. Accordingly, with virtually no opposition, in August, 1951, Congress repealed the union shop authorization election provision.

Obviously, Taft-Hartley did not turn out to be the "slave labor act" its most bitter opponents predicted. It did restrict union conduct, and, at the same time, union growth slowed significantly. But whether this was the result of the new legal restraints or more likely because of other factors, especially the growing sophistication of employer resistance, was not clear.

On the other hand, the new law also removed a mass of obstacles with which labor unions had had to contend for years. Professor Howard Lesnick has written:

> One of Professor [Paul] Hays' most prescient insights was his early recognition that the Taft-Hartley amendments would have perhaps their greatest impact in a totally unanticipated and, in a sense, perverse way. He referred to the 1947 Act as the Magna Carta of the labor movement; what he meant . . . was that the statute would ultimately free unions from the restrictions of state law and state courts, and that such a result would prove far more significant than the limited strictures newly enacted into federal law.

THE NLRB AND TAFT-HARTLEY

Taft-Hartley had a profound effect on the NLRB as an institution. Perhaps the most important change was psychological. From the outset, the Board had been charged with promoting unions and collective bargaining. There were only employer unfair labor practices under the Wagner Act, and inevitably the Board's work—however fairly and objectively performed—was perceived as prolabor. This perception was shared by labor, management, and the Board's own staff. But Taft-Hartley was unquestionably conceived as a series of restraints on unions, and, in this sense, it was designed to favor management. Thus, the Board's job after the Taft-Hartley Act was passed was more nearly in the middle of the ongoing conflict between labor and management. Both employers and unions were now subject to the NLRB's unfair labor practice powers, and neither could properly claim the agency's primary loyalty.

A few prominent members of the Board's staff resigned immediately on the enactment of Taft-Hartley, because they lacked sympathy with the law's provisions and were unwilling to aid in its administration. While their departure had little operational impact on the Board, it surely bore symbolic significance. The NLRB had lost its clear identity as an agency committed solely to promoting the organization of unions.

The enactment of Taft-Hartley also marked another kind of psychological change. The NLRB began to administer Taft-Hartley after twelve years of life. It was no longer a bold "new" agency imbued with the spirit and zeal characteristic of new agencies. It was approaching middle-aged maturity. Fewer and fewer of its staff members would recall the social and economic forces of the Depression that gave birth to the Board and its statute. There was less new ground to be broken in the law's provisions protecting the right to organize, for the Board's work had been codified in thousands of published decisions. Perhaps most significant of all, labor was no longer perceived as the underdog in a society that was becoming ever more affluent and suburban. On the contrary, social reformers now charged that labor stood in the path of social progress. American intellectuals, who had easily identified with the labor movement's aspirations in the 1930's, just as easily became disenchanted with its quite unspectacular, day-to-day work of organizing the unorganized and administering collective bargaining agreements in the late 1940's and 1950's. Labor's very successes, achieved in large measure under the umbrella protections of the Wagner Act, made it more of a middle-class, middle-of-the-road social force. The Board's salad days had come to an end.

The Board's first substantive job under Taft-Hartley was to plumb the meaning of the new law's difficult and often arcane provisions. Hundreds of test cases were tried. Dozens of new policies were promulgated. Important though this work was to the labor-management community, the public was scarcely aware that it was taking place.

Within the agency, a serious and bitter dispute broke out almost immediately between the five members and the agency's newly appointed independent general counsel, Robert Denham, who had been a trial examiner for nine years before his appointment. Although he was known to be a conservative Republican, the White House selected Denham on the theory that he sympathized with the Taft-Hartley Act and, thus, his selection would show Truman's good faith in giving substance to the will of Congress.

Denham's appointment led to both personal and philosophical conflicts with the NLRB. Denham believed and publicly proclaimed that Taft-Hartley was a "magnificent piece of legislative machinery," whereas he attacked the Wagner Act as a statute "designed and administered for the benefit of one branch of our labor-management economy, at the expense of another."

During 1948 and 1949, while the Truman Administration was committed to seeking repeal of Taft-Hartley, Denham made speeches throughout the country defending and praising the statute. Even worse, Denham publicly accused the Board of unreasonably restricting the scope of the union unfair labor practice provisions of Taft-Hartley. His actions were hardly calculated to endear him either to the White House or to the Board.

Conflicts with Denham also involved personnel matters. Immediately after enactment of Taft-Hartley, the NLRB and the general counsel entered into an agreement by which the Board delegated to him full supervisory power over the Board's regional offices. In the fall of 1949, the Board informed Denham that it wished to revise the agreement to regain its power to appoint regional directors and certain other personnel. Denham refused to relinquish the authority. Finally, in 1950, with the White House's approval, the Board made these changes in the delegation agreement unilaterally.

Perhaps in retaliation, Denham unilaterally "demoted" the Board's own solicitor and associate solicitor to the rank of assistant solicitors. The solicitor was the Board's own legal counsel, not subject to the authority of the general counsel, and the Board ignored Denham's actions accordingly.

Because of the peculiar status that Congress conferred on the general counsel, he wears several legal hats. His first responsibility is to serve as the independent prosecutor before the NLRB. After the Board has decided a case, however, the general counsel is responsible for defending the Board's decisions in the federal appellate courts. It is possible, therefore, for the general counsel to prosecute an unfair labor case on a particular theory, for the Board to reject his theory and adopt one of its own, and for the general counsel to be obliged to defend the Board's theory—not his own—in the appellate courts. In several cases, Denham severely embarrassed the Board in court by expressing the Board's official views on a legal issue and then stating his own conflicting views. This created an unseemly spectacle: The same federal agency appeared to be on different sides in the same case.

The conflicts between Denham and the Board, whose main spokesman was Chairman Paul Herzog, became so strong that communication between them was tense and unpleasant. They often exchanged harsh memoranda suggesting the other's lack of good faith and judgment.

Partly as a result of this discord, in 1950, the White House submitted to Congress Reorganization Plan XII, which would have eliminated the office of the independent general counsel and transferred his powers to the NLRB Chairman. Senator Taft led the fight against this plan, although in 1949 during the Thomas-Lesinski debates, he had been willing to transfer the general counsel's powers to the whole Board.

The now-familiar conservative coalition killed Plan XII in the Senate. The White House, organized labor, and liberal Democrats lacked the votes to overcome the opposition of management, Republicans, and conservative Southern Democrats. Having failed to eliminate Denham's job through Plan XII, the White House concluded that the conflict between Denham and the Board still must be resolved, and he was forced to resign in September, 1950. His departure was less than graceful, for in December he published a bitter article in the *Saturday Evening Post* defending the rightness of his positions and attacking his opponents.

The Denham episode was the most painful experience the NLRB ever underwent in relations with its independent general counsel. Although there were tensions between General Counsel Stuart Rothman and the Board in the late 1950's, relations otherwise have been fairly harmonious. Indeed, during the 1960's, management charged that relations between the Board and General Counsel Arnold Ordman were far too cooperative and not marked by a sufficient separation, as intended by Taft-Hartley.

Following the Presidential elections of November, 1952, Dwight D. Eisenhower entered the White House as the first Republican President in twenty years. This change in administration had a profound effect on appointments to the Board, which for its entire life had been led by members appointed by Democratic Presidents. After all, the Republican Party had historically been hostile to the Wagner Act and supportive of Taft-Hartley.

In the spring of 1953, Chairman Paul Herzog resigned from the Board and member John M. Houston's term expired. They were replaced by the first Eisenhower appointees: Guy Farmer, a former Board staff member and management lawyer in Washington, was named Chairman; Philip Ray Rodgers, chief clerk of the Senate Labor Committee during the Eightieth Congress and an adviser to Senator Taft, replaced Houston. In March, 1954, the third Eisenhower appointee, Albert C. Beeson, joined the Board. Beeson had been an industrial-relations manager for a California firm and had engaged in collective bargaining on the management side of the table.

There was now a firm Republican majority on the NLRB for the first time in its history. The "Eisenhower Board" began almost immediately to reconsider and reverse a number of precedents established by prior Boards. In most instances, these changes favored management. Now it was the labor movement's turn to complain that the Board lacked objectivity, that it was partisan in management's favor. But the management community and its organs, *The Wall Street Journal* and *Nation's Business,* joyfully announced that, for the first time in the Board's history, they were satisfied the law was being administered fairly.

Unquestionably, the Eisenhower Board made many modifications in the rulings of prior Boards. But one must remember that both the Wagner and Taft-Hartley acts conferred much discretion on the Board, particularly in fashioning appropriate bargaining units and making fact findings in unfair labor practice cases. It was the NLRB findings in precisely these areas about which the labor movement complained most bitterly during the 1950's.

One researcher, Professor Seymour Scher, published an article in 1961 that documents debates within the inner councils of the White House during the early Eisenhower years over how best to deal with the NLRB. One point of view, represented by Secretary of Commerce Sinclair Weeks and small business groups within the National Association of Manufacturers, favored elimination of the law and the Board, replacing them with state laws and an abbreviated federal statute to be administered by the federal courts. Another point of view, represented by large, national firms in the association and the U.S. Chamber of Commerce, favored retention of the Board and the statute; but these groups sought a thorough revamping of the Board's policy direction with "good" appointments. However, Professor Scher concludes, Eisenhower's advisers were so badly divided over this issue that his ultimate decision was to do nothing about the Board except to make appointments satisfactory to management. Even this decision, according to Scher, was more easily conceived than executed, for both the Labor Department and the Senate Labor Committee had something to say about NLRB appointments. Eisenhower's third appointee, Albert Beeson, won Senate approval only by a squeak, forty-five to forty-two, following a 3-week committee review of his qualifications and a Senate debate in which Senator John F. Kennedy, among others, challenged his suitability for appointment. After the Beeson confirmation struggle, the White House was far more circumspect about its appointments.*

In a later chapter we shall return to examine the impact of national politics on the Board and its work. It is by no means a one-sided issue, for many thoughtful critics believe that the regulatory agencies should reflect in some measure the vicissitudes in the White House. Others disagree, particularly when it comes to the NLRB.

---

* John H. Fanning, a Democrat, was appointed to the NLRB by President Eisenhower in 1957. Fanning had been a career federal executive. He is the only Eisenhower appointee to be reappointed by subsequent Presidents. Indeed, he has been reappointed successively by Presidents Kennedy, Johnson, and Nixon.

IV

The Landrum-Griffin Act and After

The American labor movement reached its postwar nadir during 1957 and 1958. In these years, the Senate Select Committee on Improper Activities in the Labor or Management Field—better known as the McClellan committee—conducted a long series of hearings that exposed scandalous misconduct by certain union officers and management representatives.

THE McCLELLAN COMMITTEE AND LANDRUM-GRIFFIN

In 1955–56 hearings, a Senate committee under the guidance of Senator Paul H. Douglas had revealed serious abuses in the administration of union welfare and pension funds. This investigation led to the enactment of disclosure legislation and prompted the recently merged AFL-CIO to establish an Ethical Practices Committee, which moved to check and then expel affiliated unions accused of corruption. But these modest reforms merely set the stage for the more sweeping disclosures to come.

Testimony before the McClellan committee revealed that some unions engaged in violent interference with the democratic rights of their members, followed highly irregular election practices, misused union funds for personal gain, imposed trusteeship or supervision over local unions for improper reasons, employed officials with criminal records, failed to maintain reasonable records, and engaged in a variety of other abuses of trust. There was also evidence that certain management representatives made a business of bribing union officers and of reprehensible practices to subvert the right of employees to select unions and officers of their choice.

It was in these hearings that a little-known official of the Teamsters Union, James Riddle Hoffa, first came to public attention in confrontations with the committee's young chief counsel, Robert Kennedy. His brother, John Fitzgerald Kennedy, the future President, served on the McClellan committee. And it was also in these hearings that an obscure management "consultant" from Chicago, Nathan Shefferman, was exposed to public view. Shefferman's name has ever since been synonymous with the notorious practices in which he specialized: bribing union officials and engaging in industrial espionage to protect his clients—including the giant Sears, Roebuck chain —from legitimate union organizing campaigns.

Of course, corruption and misconduct were not typical of the labor movement or of the management community. But the McClellan committee's revelations satisfied Congress and the informed public that this problem was sufficiently grave to justify extensive legislation regulating the internal affairs of labor organizations and the practices of management representatives.

Beginning in 1958, a fascinating legislative battle unfolded in the Congress over the need for new labor legislation. The McClellan committee had focused mainly on abuses by unions in their internal affairs. There was, however, a significant amount of evidence that some unions used the traditional economic weapons of labor, particularly the picket line, for improper purposes. For this reason, although there was general agreement in Congress that *some* regulation of internal union affairs was warranted, many congressmen also believed that reform legislation should include amendments to Taft-Hartley to deal with perceived abuses of economic power by unions. A relatively mild "disclosure" bill was introduced and passed in the Senate in 1958, but it died in the House. Labor, which had a strategy of opposing any bill that did not include "sweeteners" to favorably amend Taft-Hartley, was unenthusiastic about this bill. Management also opposed it, because it did not strengthen Taft-Hartley enough to suit employers. In retrospect, it is obvious that organized labor made a serious strategic mistake; by insisting on prolabor Taft-Hartley Amendments, it opened the door to amendments that it would find unacceptable.

Public interest in labor reform legislation reached a peak in 1959. For many months, there was intense lobbying by labor and employer groups in the Congress to influence the outcome of pending legislation. Certainly, it was the fiercest legislative struggle over labor policy since the fight over Taft-Hartley.

In the end, after an extraordinary succession of legislative maneuvers, which included major amendments made on the floor of the Senate itself, Congress enacted a statute with the mouth-filling name of the Labor-Management Reporting and Disclosure Act of 1959. It is generally known as the Landrum-Griffin Act, after the names of its House sponsors. This law has seven titles or major divisions. The first six titles deal primarily with internal union affairs and are administered by the U.S. Department of Labor. The seventh title contains amendments to Taft-Hartley, and it is those with which the NLRB is concerned.

The Landrum-Griffin Act amended Taft-Hartley in these seven major respects:

1. *Secondary boycotts.* Since 1947, Taft-Hartley's secondary boycott provisions had undergone detailed interpretation by the Board and the federal courts in a variety of factual contexts. Reviewing these interpretations, Congress concluded that there were significant loopholes in Taft-Hartley's prohibi-

tion of secondary boycotts. Landrum-Griffin closed these loopholes through a series of amendments to Section 8(b) (4) and through the addition of a new unfair labor practice prohibition against so-called hot cargo agreements (under which employers bound themselves in advance to boycott any other employers with whom the union had a dispute), Section 8(e).

2. *Organization and recognition picketing.* The McClellan committee received evidence that some unions used the picket line as an economic weapon to require employees to join unions against their will (organization picketing) and in other instances to require employers to force their employees to join unions (recognition picketing). The issue of picketing by labor organizations had grown legally complex under federal and state laws over the years, and, in Landrum-Griffin, the Congress undertook to regulate the permissible limits of picketing in considerable detail. It did so through a complex new unfair labor practice prohibition against unions, Section 8(b) (7).

3. *Prehire agreements.* It had long been recognized that the building and construction industry is different from most other industries, in the sense that employees in this industry commonly work for a single employer for only a few weeks or months and then move on to another construction project and a new employer. Under Taft-Hartley, it was illegal for employers to sign so-called prehire agreements with construction industry unions, although the law was honored largely in the breach. Congress, in the Landrum-Griffin Act, enacted a special exception for the construction industry: It permitted prehire agreements in special circumstances and also permitted union security agreements under which workers may be required to join a union after seven days' initial employment, rather than the standard thirty days permitted by Taft-Hartley. These provisions constituted a new Section 8(f).

4. *Voting by economic strikers.* The Taft-Hartley Act, as interpreted, often deprived economic strikers, who protested wages and working conditions, of the right to vote in

NLRB elections conducted while a strike was in progress. This had the practical effect of disenfranchising strikers, while permitting strike replacements and nonstriking employees to vote. The manifest inequity of this result led Congress to amend Section 9(c) (3) of Taft-Hartley to allow economic strikers, as well as strike replacements and nonstrikers, to vote in elections, subject to regulations to be promulgated by the Board. This was perhaps the most important "sweetener" in Landrum-Griffin from labor's point of view.

5. *Delegation to regional directors.* Under the Wagner and Taft-Hartley acts only the NLRB in Washington could determine bargaining units and direct representation or other kinds of elections. When the Board's case load was small, the agency was able to process representation cases within reasonable time limits. Beginning in 1957, however, the Board's case load began to grow enormously; delays in processing election cases became longer and longer, sometimes requiring half a year or more for even routine election petitions. Everyone in the labor-management community agreed that such delays were intolerable and inconsistent with the aims of the law. Responding to this crisis in the NLRB's administration of the election provisions of the law, Congress authorized the Board to delegate most of its power to define bargaining units and to direct elections to its regional directors, subject to a discretionary review before the whole Board.

In 1961, the Board finally delegated election powers to regional directors under an elaborate set of rules and regulations. Regional directors have acted under their delegated authority with such energy and good sense that election procedures have improved vastly, to the evident satisfaction of all. The impact of the delegation of authority was greatest on the relatively routine cases, which could be decided under clear precedents. The Board retained authority to decide novel and important cases, as well as cases in which one of the parties believed that a regional director had made an error of fact or law. Not only has this new process speeded up the conduct of elections, it has also relieved the Board of the crushing burden of deciding hundreds of routine cases, allowing more time to be spent on important new issues.

6. *Non-Communist affidavit provisions repealed.* The non-Communist affidavit provisions of Taft-Hartley and the related reporting provisions had become virtually meaningless over the years as a result of judicial interpretation. Accordingly, Congress repealed Sections 9(f), 9(g), and 9(h) entirely. These provisions were reincorporated, however, in a much stronger fashion in the other sections of the Landrum-Griffin Act, administered by the Department of Labor.

7. *No-man's-land problem solved.* A series of Supreme Court decisions during the 1950's established a complex principle known as "federal pre-emption" in the labor-relations field. In essence, these decisions ruled that Congress had occupied the whole field of labor relations in interstate commerce through comprehensive regulation by the Taft-Hartley Act. Under the "supremacy clause" of the Constitution, when Congress occupies a legislative field, the individual states may not simultaneously exercise regulatory power that might conflict with congressional regulation. The Supreme Court ruled, therefore, that state courts and agencies were "pre-empted" from applying their own regulatory policies to interstate labor relations in situations where the NLRB had the power to act, *even though the Board might voluntarily decline to exercise its regulatory power.* This created a "no-man's-land" problem in cases where the NLRB *would not act*—perhaps because the employer was very small—but where the pre-emption doctrine precluded state regulation. In other words, the NLRB *would* not and the states *could* not act. Landrum-Griffin solved this problem by providing that state courts and agencies could regulate those interstate labor disputes that the NLRB refused to take. However, to preclude the Board from erasing the Taft-Hartley Act by declining to exercise its jurisdiction over broad classes of labor disputes, Landrum-Griffin also

provided that the Board may not refuse to accept those cases that it would have taken under the jurisdictional standards prevailing on August 1, 1959.

Like Taft-Hartley, Landrum-Griffin was a legislative response to perceived abuses of union power. But the new legislation made only relatively minor changes in the fundamental structure of the federal labor laws erected by the Wagner and Taft-Hartley acts.

THE NLRB IN THE 1960's AND 1970's

Throughout the 1950's the Board followed a generally conservative path. Organized labor protested that the NLRB had become an instrument of oppression, that it perverted Congress's purposes by misinterpretations. Of course, the management community disagreed vigorously.

When John F. Kennedy entered the White House in 1961, the Board once again faced the imminent prospect of a change in membership. Kennedy had received substantial support from the labor movement in his successful campaign against Richard M. Nixon. Hence, it seemed likely that the new President would be sympathetic to labor.

The record of the Eisenhower Board was scrutinized in lengthy hearings by a Select Subcommittee of the House of Representatives on the National Labor Relations Board beginning in March, 1961. This committee, chaired by Representative Roman C. Pucinski of Illinois, had its genesis in strong appeals by labor to survey the current shortcomings of the Act and its administration. Because the committee was dominated by liberal Democrats close to the labor movement, it is hardly surprising that its final report was sharply critical of the Eisenhower Board and accurately reflected the labor movement's dissatisfaction with Board policies of the 1950's. Eight years later a Senate subcommittee chaired by Senator

Sam Ervin of North Carolina would engage in an equally vigorous critique of the 1960's Board from a management point of view.

Notwithstanding the bias of many of the witnesses before the Pucinski committee, the group's final report made recommendations that fairly exposed serious problems in the Board's administration that had long been the source of criticism by objective students of the Board's work, particularly the problems of delay and poor internal management.

On March 7, 1961, President Kennedy made his first NLRB appointment: Frank W. McCulloch of Illinois, a lawyer and long-time administrative assistant to Senator Paul H. Douglas. McCulloch was also designated as Chairman of the Board, replacing Boyd Leedom of North Dakota who continued to serve as a member for two years. One month later, the second Kennedy appointment was made: Gerald A. Brown of California, a career NLRB official who had served for many years as regional director of the Board's San Francisco office.

In 1962, the President reappointed John Fanning for a second term, and in August, 1963, Howard Jenkins, Jr., of Colorado joined the Board. He was a prominent Labor Department lawyer, a Republican, and the Board's first black member. Finally, in 1965, President Johnson appointed Sam Zagoria of New Jersey, a distinguished journalist and administrative assistant to Senator Clifford Case of New Jersey.

These five men—McCulloch, Brown, Fanning, Jenkins, and Zagoria—constituted the Kennedy-Johnson or "New Frontier" NLRB.

In May, 1963, Arnold Ordman was appointed as the agency's independent general counsel. Ordman had been a career attorney at the National Labor Relations Board, most recently having served as a trial examiner and as Chairman McCulloch's chief counsel. Throughout the decade bonds of personal friendship and respect between the Board and the general counsel produced relations that were remarkably harmonious and cooperative. He scrupulously maintained his independence and separation from the Board in performing his prosecutorial duties. At the same time, he recognized the primary authority of the Board to interpret the law and frankly avowed the need for cooperation with it. "We work under the same statute and we have a common purpose—to further the policy of the act," he told a House committee in 1966. His proven competence and commitment gave spirit to the field and enforcement staffs under his direction and helped to lift all operations to new levels.

If the Eisenhower Board can fairly be characterized as generally conservative, noninnovative, and promanagement, the Kennedy-Johnson Board might perhaps be considered generally liberal, innovative, and—if not prolabor—strongly supportive of employee rights and the philosophy of free collective bargaining. Obviously, such characterizations are simplistic and basically unfair to individuals. Fanning and Jenkins, for example, brought a strong sense of traditional legal reasoning to the Board. McCulloch and Brown often voted together, as a minority, in favor of new approaches to old problems with less concern for traditional legal norms. Zagoria, who was not a lawyer but a writer and an acute observer of Capitol Hill, brought to the Board an intelligent generalist's breadth of vision, as well as a strong sense of direction for good public policy.

None of the members of the Kennedy-Johnson Board had served as a labor or management representative in collective bargaining. Hence, professional labor-relations technocrats occasionally complained that this Board lacked a sense of "realism" about labor-management problems. Defenders replied, however, that the Board members were not encumbered by the partisanship that was characteristic of several members of the Eisenhower Board. On a number of basic issues, the "new" Board in the 1960's did reconsider and reverse past interpretations of the statute, most notably in the areas of appropriate bargaining units, determination of union majorities by authorization cards, the scope of the duty to bargain, organizational picketing, and stronger remedies. Reviewing courts upheld most of these interpretations.

Much has been written about the Kennedy-Johnson Board and its work, and in later chapters we shall discuss several of its leading decisions. Throughout its term, this Board's case load continued to rise dramatically, and it constantly struggled to maintain and improve its case handling procedures.

In 1963, an employer-financed group published a lengthy volume by a management attorney entitled *The New Frontier NLRB*. The book defined the new, hard line of management opposition to the Board, charging that "the Kennedy majority [to be distinguished from the remaining Eisenhower appointees] is undermining the purpose of the statute, frustrating the intent of Congress, and demoralizing major areas of labor-management relations." Of course, almost precisely the same criticism had been made of the Eisenhower Board by labor in the hearings of the Pucinski committee in 1961, but this book charged that it was *only* during the Eisenhower years that the statute was fairly administered. Variations on these themes were subsequently developed by a self-styled "Labor Law Reform" group, made up of lawyers for many of the country's leading industrial concerns. They have actively opposed some nominees for Board membership and proposed voluminous amendments to the law to reverse unwanted Board and court interpretations.

The drumbeat of management criticism reached a climax in 1968 when the Senate Judiciary Subcommittee on the Separation of Powers, chaired by long-time Board critic Senator Sam Ervin of North Carolina,* held a series of hear-

---

* Senator Ervin is an interesting and complex man. On labor and race issues, his record is quite conservative. He has established a strong record as a civil libertarian, however. In the labor-relations field, he has been a defender of North Carolina's textile management interests, and in this role he even argued a case against the NLRB before the Supreme Court in 1965, a rare action by a U.S. senator in the twentieth century. His place in history will probably be indentified with his chairmanship of the Senate hearings on the "Watergate" scandal in 1973.

ings on the Board's work under the rubric of studying whether regulatory agencies were violating the Constitutional separation of powers. The committee was hostile to the Board, a fact it took few pains to conceal, but such partisanship is not unusual on the part of congressional committees. To its credit, the Ervin committee called management, union, and academic witnesses to testify about the Board's performance, even though the committee's final report reflected the views of those who were critical of the Board, ignoring those who had anything good to say about it.

The management witnesses were all hostile; the union witnesses were generally friendly; and the academic witnesses —who had no partisan axes to grind—were largely supportive of the Board's work. Notable among the academic witnesses was Derek Bok, then dean of the Harvard Law School and now Harvard's president. He emphasized that the polarized, partisan atmosphere of American labor relations has always resulted in unbalanced criticism of agencies charged with carrying out Congress's labor policies, and he added:

> One can find other highly industrialized democratic countries in which the principal labor court or regulatory body has been met not with criticism, but with universal acclaim by both sides, labor and management. This has not been true in this country, and I would suggest that the underlying causes for the reaction to the Board's work, and the problems under which it labors, are probably rooted in our industrial relations system, and in particular in two factors which are hallmarks of our industrial relations system. One is the fact that we have by comparison with other industrialized countries a very high degree of hostility that permeates our labor relations.
>
> The other factor is by comparison with other countries we have an extremely decentralized process of collective bargaining and labor relations in which there is . . . comparatively little industrywide bargaining. The bulk of our labor relations are worked out on an individual basis in separate plants and separate companies. . . .
>
> One result is that enormous burdens are placed in our system

on the process of lawmaking. Because of hostility and the lack of strong central bodies on either side, there is very little co-operation in settling basic conflicts of value and principle that emerge in labor relations. In other countries you can find agreements by labor and management to settle such issues as strikes, recognition, representation rights, retaliation by em-ployers and so forth. These efforts have never come to much in this country. . . . As a result almost all basic conflicts of value and interest and principle in the field of labor relations are handed over to our lawmaking processes, which is a rather heavy burden to bear.

Internally, during the 1960's, the agency enjoyed high staff morale. For most of the decade, there was unprecedented continuity in Board leadership. McCulloch, Brown, Fanning, and Jenkins were all reappointed to second terms, as was General Counsel Ordman. Relations between the general counsel and the Board were consistently friendly, and rela-tions among the five members—who sharply disagreed on a variety of statutory issues—were cordial and cooperative as well. Some NLRB staff members speak of the 1960's as a period during which an unusually friendly tone prevailed in Board offices and in the relations among the Board, the general counsel, and the field offices.*

As the White House changed hands in 1969, the Board once again faced changes in membership. Sam Zagoria's term expired in December, 1969, and, though a Republican, he was not reappointed by President Nixon. Zagoria was succeeded by the first Nixon appointee, Edward B. Miller of Illinois, who was designated as Chairman. Miller had been a successful management attorney in Chicago for twenty years before his appointment, and organized labor immediately charged

---

* On the other hand, shortly after President Kennedy issued Executive Order 10988 in 1962, which authorized federal employees to organize and engage in collective bargaining, many of the Board's employees joined unions and negotiated contracts with the Board. As an employer, the Board had its full share of managerial problems and was several times red-faced at charges by its own employees that it had not bargained in good faith.

that the White House was again attempting to stack the Board with biased appointees. Labor backed away from a full fight over his confirmation, however, and Miller was easily confirmed by the Senate.

In his first speech as Board Chairman, Miller attempted to allay fears that he was a management partisan or that his predecessors on the 1960's Board had been partisan and biased. He commented:

> So long as a basic air of controversy exists, any agency charged with decision making and law enforcement is bound to be accused of favoring one side or the other. Losing parties are, of course, the principal purveyors of such criticism. If you were to examine the transcripts of the various rounds of hearings in the Congress which have dealt with the activities of this agency, you would find that a very heavy proportion of the testimony is invariably offered by persons who have had matters decided adversely to them by this Board. The surprising thing is, sometimes, that this criticism from hard losers is taken so seriously, but that may be due to the fact that the continuing controversy spills over into the political area, and tales of abuse by employers or unions—particularly big employers or big unions— are apparently good grist for the mill of campaign oratory.
>
> But blanket accusations that Board members are the stooges of either labor unions or employers are in my view absurd.

Chairman Miller was joined by two additional Nixon appointees, both career NLRB officials: Ralph Kennedy had been the agency's regional director in Los Angeles, and John ("Doc") Penello had been regional director in Baltimore. In December, 1972, John H. Fanning's third term expired. To the general applause of the labor-management community, he was reappointed by President Nixon to an unprecedented fourth term. Similarly, in August, 1973, Howard Jenkins, Jr., was reappointed to a third term. For the office of general counsel, to succeed Arnold Ordman, in August, 1971, the President appointed Peter G. Nash, the highly respected solicitor in the Department of Labor, with prior labor-law experience, mostly representing employers in Rochester, New York.

The Nixon NLRB, contrary to labor's worst fears and management's highest hopes, has not engaged in any systematic program to reverse prior Board precedents on a wholesale basis. Nevertheless, the Board has undoubtedly moved in a generally more conservative direction, and once again *The Wall Street Journal* finds occasional decisions that it can regard as "properly" decided. It is of course too early to make any serious assessment of the work of the Nixon Board, although several of its leading decisions will be analyzed in later chapters.

THE POSTAL REORGANIZATION ACT OF 1970

The NLRB unexpectedly received a significant addition to its responsibilities in 1970. In the spring of 1969, President Nixon proposed a reorganization plan for the U.S. Post Office Department to transfer its functions to an independent public corporation. This proposal was effectively opposed by the powerful postal unions, which were dissatisfied with the plan's labor-relations provisions.

Then, in February, 1970, a nationwide postal strike nearly paralyzed the economy. In a complex strike settlement, the postal unions agreed to support Nixon's reorganization plan in exchange for favorable labor provisions. These provisions, embodied in the Postal Reorganization Act of 1970, apply most of the representation and unfair labor practice provisions of the Taft-Hartley Act to the new U.S. Postal Service.

By this Act, Congress added 750,000 postal employees to the NLRB's statutory jurisdiction, but the Board's fears that this expanded area of activity might potentially overwhelm it with new kinds of public sector labor-relations problems are apparently unjustified in practice.

With this example before them, a number of other federal employee labor organizations have sought coverage by the

NLRB as well, but there seems to be little likelihood that Congress will respond to these wishes in the near future. In 1972, Congressman Frank Thompson, Jr., of New Jersey introduced a bill to bring state and local government employees under the NLRB's jurisdiction and conducted hearings on it and companion bills. The probability of such a tidal wave of additional Board work is no doubt slight, unless, contrary to the prevailing trend, a substantial number of states and localities leave without legal protections their employees' rights to organize and bargain collectively.

Legislation to bring nonprofit hospital employees under the Board's jurisdiction, however, was winning impressive support, including that of the Administration, in mid-1973; and some new groups joined the push for similar coverage for farm workers, hoping to reduce the violent conflicts in the vineyards and lettuce fields of the Far West.

V

Organization and Procedures

When Taft-Hartley separated the NLRB investigatory and prosecutory functions from its adjudicatory functions in 1947, the effect was to create two agencies within one. And, as indicated in previous chapters, the separation mandated by Taft-Hartley between the Board and its general counsel has occasionally led to sharp policy conflicts between them.

THE GENERAL COUNSEL'S OFFICE

Most NLRB general counsel have attempted to follow the law as interpreted by the Board and the federal appellate courts with great fidelity. Particularly in recent years, a tradition has emerged in which the general counsel has pledged to follow the law when it is clear and settled and, when it is unclear, to bring all unresolved problems to the Board for resolution.

This philosophy was well stated by General Counsel George Bott before a congressional committee in 1953:

> The separate prosecutor by probing the law at its outermost limits may continuously present the judicial arm with situations which challenge its past theories from a new perspective. This exploration of the law and this challenge of the judicial inter-

pretations under it provide full assurance that the intent of Congress will be effectuated. Moreover, the General Counsel, by issuing complaints which explore the periphery of the law, offers to the parties an opportunity to obtain full consideration of their positions not only before the Board but in the courts.

In colloquy with General Counsel Arnold Ordman in 1968, Senator Sam Ervin observed that the Taft-Hartley Act

. . . makes the Office of the General Counsel an office of very high importance. As I understand the act, the Board has no authority to hear any unfair labor charge or any allegation of an unfair labor practice unless the General Counsel issues a complaint. The General Counsel is not only independent of the Board. It is also independent of the demands of the employers who may claim that they have been unjustly affected by events, and independent of the unions and the individual employees. They have no access to the Board or the processes of law except through the General Counsel. So the General Counsel does have, I would say, almost as omnipotent authority as the laws of the United States have ever vested in any single individual who is the occupant of a public office.

To this General Counsel Ordman replied: "It is a job, Mr. Chairman, calculated to create unpopularity."

To carry out his investigatory and prosecutory functions, the general counsel has both a large headquarters staff in Washington and a substantial field staff. Over the years, the general counsel has carried out a series of internal reorganizations. The most recent reorganization took place in July, 1972, and the changes made then are discussed below.

The Washington Headquarters

The general counsel's Washington, D.C., office is located in the same building with those of the Board, which, at the moment, are in a multistory office building leased from a private owner.

The general counsel's Washington office is a nerve center of activity. Few novel decisions are made in the field offices without prior approval from Washington. The Washington office is currently organized into four major divisions, each of which is headed by an associate general counsel or assistant general counsel:

A *Division of Operations Management* coordinates case handling activities in the field, supervises day-to-day field work, and develops systems for more effective case handling.

A *Division of Advice* provides guidance to regional offices in cases concerning new or unusually complex issues. It also has responsibility for the general counsel's research activities and special projects.

An *Office of Appeals* is a special judicial body within the general counsel's office. Its function is to review and advise the general counsel with respect to appeals from the refusal of a regional director to issue an unfair labor practice complaint. The work of this office gives parties an extra measure of due process in assuring that unfair labor practice charges are closely scrutinized.

A *Division of Enforcement Litigation* enforces and defends the Board's orders in the federal appellate courts. It is also charged with handling contempt cases and miscellaneous litigation affecting the Board. Several appellate judges have stated that in their experience the briefs prepared for the Board by this division are the best government briefs they receive.

The offices mentioned above are concerned with discharging the general counsel's duties to administer substantive provisions of the law. Another office supervised by the general counsel, the *Division of Administration,* is the agency's main housekeeping office. Its duties include budget preparation and management, personnel administration, finance, organization, methods, and administrative statistics. Although the Division of Administration is supervised by the general counsel, its responsibility is to perform services of a housekeeping nature for the entire agency, the Board, and its members, as well as for the general counsel's office.

The Regional Offices

The Board maintains thirty-one regional offices and twelve subregional or resident offices in major cities. Regional offices are headed by a regional director who supervises a staff that includes a regional attorney and a number of trial attorneys, field examiners, and clericals. The general counsel supervises these offices.

All case activity is initiated and investigated in the regional offices, which employ approximately 1,600 people. It is these staff members who "meet the public" and perform the bulk of the NLRB's vital day-to-day work. In these offices almost 14,000 election petitions and 27,000 unfair labor practice cases are now processed annually under procedures outlined later in this chapter. Hearings, consent agreements, elections, investigations, settlements, and trials are the grist of the regional office mills. Moreover, these offices are responsible for policing compliance with NLRB and court orders and settlement agreements. They prosecute injunctions in the federal district courts, as well.

To the great credit of the regional offices, they have successfully pursued settlement programs and election agreements to secure voluntary compliance with the statute without the need for formal litigation. Five out of six probable violation cases, for example, are settled in the regional offices. And 90 per cent of all unfair labor practice cases are normally disposed of within a period of forty-five days—a remarkable record of administrative efficiency. Consent agreements are obtained for four out of five elections.

THE BOARD'S OFFICES

The Board's five members have offices only in Washington, D.C.

The Board Members. Each Board member, including the Chairman, has a staff of approximately twenty-five legal assistants who work solely for him. They assist in reviewing transcripts, studying the applicable law, and writing decisions. Each member also has a small clerical staff and a chief counsel, essentially a staff director who supervises the work of the legal assistants. The chief counsel is assisted by an associate chief counsel. Without impairing the collegial quality of the five Board members and their staffs working together, each staff under the guidance of its Board member is a separate, vital institution: Within it intensive study, analysis, and discussion take place to assist the central process under which Board members issue about 1,400 decisions in contested cases annually.

The NLRB Chairman. Under Taft-Hartley, the NLRB Chairman has no independent powers that he does not share in equal measure with the other members of the Board. He is, in short, the first among equals. Traditionally, however, the Chairman has enjoyed certain intangible authority as the Presidentially designated presiding officer of the Board. This embraces added responsibilities for presenting, along with the general counsel, the agency's budget and appropriations request, appearing before congressional committees, representing the Board in interagency matters, and handling day-to-day administrative problems. (The late Chairman Boyd Leedom estimated that these matters consumed 50 per cent of his time.) Of course, the Chairman performs various honorific duties as the titular head of the agency, but he does not possess independent administrative authority that chairmen of several regulatory agencies have been granted by Congress. And on every issue of substance, including all matters of agency management, the Chairman has only one vote to cast: all Board members take part in the decision.

The Executive Secretary. Because Board members perform judicial functions, it is improper for parties involved in pending cases to speak or communicate *ex parte* with any member or legal assistant. Anyone wishing to contact the Board or any of its members about a pending case must do so through the office of the executive secretary, which was specially created to deal with the public. In addition, the secretary is the Board's chief administrative and judicial management officer, in charge of such matters as handling formal correspondence with private parties, other agencies, and members of Congress; preparing the Board's dockets; coordinating the Board's case load and work flow; maintaining formal records of Board actions; and the like. As a practical matter, the executive secretary's office is a vital one, because of its enormous responsibility for internal administration of the Board's case work. In recent decades, the Board has selected as its executive secretary outstanding civil servants who have performed their sensitive duties with great distinction, despite changes in political administration and changes in the substance of the law. One would be hard pressed to identify career federal executives who have served their agencies with greater fidelity and skill than the Board's former executive secretary, Ogden W. Fields, and its current executive secretary, John Truesdale.

The Solicitor. Although each Board member has a chief counsel and about twenty-five lawyers on his personal staff, the Board also has an institutional legal adviser, the solicitor, who advises the Board with respect to pending cases, proposed rules and regulations, and a host of other matters. When the general counsel recommends that the Board seek or decline to seek Supreme Court review of a case decided by a federal appellate court, it is the solicitor who makes an independent study of the general counsel's recommendation for the Board. In recent years, the solicitor has been assigned responsibility for writing advisory opinions for the Board, a relatively new procedure. However, because of the vast authority conferred by Taft-Hartley on the Board's general counsel and because each Board member has a staff of lawyers to advise him on technical matters, the solicitor's role is a limited one.

The Division of Information. This office prepares press releases and cooperates with media interested in the agency's work. While most of the Board's work is far from newsworthy, it is nonetheless important to the specialized reporting organizations and publications that supply news of the NLRB to persons interested in the labor-relations field. A very few Board decisions are even of national importance and may make headlines across the country. This office also prepares a weekly summary of the Board's work, as well as a variety of specialized publications about the Board.

The Division of Judges. Administrative law judges (until 1972 known as trial examiners) are hearing officers of the Board who preside over unfair labor practice proceedings and make recommendations of fact and law to the Board. They are appointed by the Board from lists of qualified applicants compiled by the Civil Service Commission. Under the Administrative Procedure Act of 1946, administrative law judges—who have few of the Constitutional trappings of other federal judges, such as Presidential appointment, Senate confirmation, lifetime tenure, and the like—are insulated from contact with other staff members of the agencies they serve in order to assure the impartiality of their work. Many administrative law judges are career agency employees who have served as attorneys on the staffs of Board members or the general counsel; others have been appointed following careers as union or management attorneys. With few exceptions, administrative law judges have served the agency and the public with distinction and imagination. The corps has included former Board members, agency general counsel, solicitors, chief counsel to Board members, and others who, like Arthur Leff, have achieved well-deserved national reputations for their scholarship.

Most administrative law judges are stationed in Washington and are dispatched by a chief judge to hearings throughout the country. Twenty judges stationed in San Francisco preside over West Coast cases.

Although administrative law judges are well paid—their GS-16 ratings earn them upwards of $31,500 annually—the

Left: Senator Robert F. Wagner authored the National Labor Relations Act of 1935, which climaxed more than a century of struggle over the rights of workers. (AFL-CIO News *photo*)

Below: A Fort Wayne, Indiana, firehouse was the site of the first NLRB election, December 12, 1935.

Senator Robert A. Taft, principal author of the Taft-Hartley Act of 1947, testifies before a Senate committee against President Truman's unsuccessful plan to abolish the post of independent prosecutor and counsel for the NLRB.

Strikes and confrontation were common in the early days of the fight for union recognition and representation. Here, striking truck drivers battle Minneapolis police in June, 1934.

Police disperse pickets at the South Chicago works of Republic Steel in 1937, leaving ten dead and scores wounded in the "Memorial Day Massacre." (*Photo from Archives of Labor History and Urban Affairs, Wayne State University*)

Above: Sit-down strikers at the Detroit Chrysler-Dodge plant in March, 1937, gather around their crudely constructed cannon as more than twenty thousand union sympathizers demonstrate in the street. (*Photo from Archives of Labor History and Urban Affairs, Wayne State University*)

Below: Violence flares on the picket line in the 1949 Bell Aircraft strike.

The United Electrical Radio and Machine Workers of America, CIO, files a petition for an NLRB election at the Sperry Gyroscope Company in 1942. (AFL-CIO News *photo*)

Other AFL-CIO unions support the Rubber Workers in a 1967 election at the Mattel Company toy plants in California. (AFL-CIO News *photo*)

Voters' names are checked against an eligibility list during a 1943 election at a Sherwin-Williams Defense Corporation plant.

Contested ballots in a longshoremen's representation election are counted by NLRB representatives as members of the concerned unions look on. (AFL-CIO News *photo*)

Jubilant members of the Washington, D.C., Teachers Local 6 celebrate their April, 1967, victory over the D.C. Education Association for bargaining rights for 6,727 public school teachers. (AFL-CIO News *photo*)

Left: Southern textile workers, discharged for union activity, protest NLRB delays in obtaining action on their case. (*Textile Workers Union of America photo*)

Below: Frank McCulloch, co-author of this book, chaired the controversial Kennedy-Johnson NLRB.

This cartoon from the *Wall Street Journal* finds the Board sympathetic to labor rather than management. (*Reprinted by permission*)

"I DON'T SUPPOSE YOU HAVE ONE SAYING SOMETHING LIKE 'SORRY ABOUT THAT NLRB DECISION'?"

The 1973–74 National Labor Relations Board included, left to right, Ralph Kennedy, John Fanning, Chairman Edward Miller, Howard Jenkins, and John Penello.

A 1967 cake-cutting ceremony marks the twenty-five millionth ballot in NLRB elections. Left to right are George Meany, AFL-CIO president; Leonard P. Scheno, Steelworkers Union; and William F. May, National Association of Manufacturers. Scheno represents the twenty-five millionth secret-ballot voter. (AFL-CIO News *photo*)

Florence Daley, illegally discharged from her job with Erie Technological Products, Inc., was awarded $18,700 in back pay by the NLRB.

In marked contrast to early labor-management strife, representatives of General Motors and the United Auto Workers begin successful negotiations in 1973. (*Photo from Archives of Labor History and Urban Affairs, Wayne State University*)

Cesar Chavez and members of the United Farm Workers, not covered by the provisions of the National Labor Relations Act, continue the struggle for workers' rights. The big question: Will the Act be amended to cover farm workers, public employees, and nonprofit hospital employees, who are now excluded?

agency has recently had difficulty in finding a sufficient number of qualified applicants. Currently, the Board employs about a hundred administrative law judges.

PROCEDURES IN UNFAIR LABOR PRACTICE CASES

The NLRB has no authority to initiate unfair labor practice cases. Its machinery may be invoked only by the filing of a formal "charge" that alleges that an employer or labor organization has committed an unfair labor practice. But literally *any* person may file an unfair labor practice charge with the Board, whether or not he has any personal interest in the outcome.

Charges may be filed in any of the Board's forty-three field offices. Upon receipt of a new charge, a field examiner or attorney is assigned to conduct an investigation of the facts, which normally will include an interview with all named parties and with knowledgeable witnesses. Of course, any person who wishes to present testimony or arguments concerning a case under investigation will be heard by the field examiner. Upon completion of a field investigation, the examiner recommends to the regional director either issuance of an unfair labor practice complaint or dismissal of the charge. Although the regional director is technically empowered to make this decision himself, in most regional offices a panel of experienced regional office personnel will commonly review the field examiner's report and, in turn, make its own recommendation to the regional director.

If the regional director decides to *dismiss* a charge, this generally closes the door on a case. The person who filed the charge—the "charging party"—has only one recourse: He may appeal to the Office of Appeals within the general counsel's office in Washington. Although this right of appeal is an important safeguard against arbitrary conduct by regional directors, it is only in rare cases—roughly one out of twenty—that the general counsel, acting with the advice of his Office of Appeals, reverses a regional director's decision. The general counsel's authority is absolute and final with respect to the issuance of unfair labor practice complaints, and in this context some experts regard the general counsel as a "labor czar," for he may exercise his far-reaching powers without review or redress. These powers, however, are like those of any public prosecutor. Someone must sift the cases that reveal probable violations from those that do not. The rarity—indeed, the almost total absence—of claims that the general counsel's exercise of his power has been arbitrary or capricious testifies to the effectiveness of the internal appeals procedure, unique among federal agencies, described above. Professor Kenneth Culp Davis of the University of Chicago Law School has written, "Altogether, the system of the NLRB General Counsel is deserving of admiration. It is surely worthy of study by other prosecutors."

If the regional director's review of the field investigation persuades him that a violation of the law has occurred, he will issue an unfair labor practice complaint against the person alleged to have violated the law, the "respondent." This formal *complaint* by a regional director sets in motion the prosecutory apparatus of the statute. The respondent is required to answer the complaint, admitting or denying its allegations.

Fortunately, in the great majority of cases, the respondent agrees to settle the complaint without the necessity of a formal hearing. For practical purposes, however, a settlement before a formal hearing usually results in the same kind of remedy that the Board itself would have directed, if it had found a violation. In discriminatory discharge cases, for example, a settlement typically requires the employer to reinstate the victim of discrimination with back pay and to post a notice. To encourage settlements, however, the general counsel normally will accept somewhat "easier" terms in earlier stages of a case and will demand somewhat "harder" terms for a settlement in more advanced stages. Thus, in an early stage of the complaint the general counsel may not require the settlement order to be enforced by a court decree; later, he may.

If the respondent does not choose to settle the general counsel's complaint, a formal hearing is scheduled before an administrative law judge in the community in which the alleged unfair labor practice case arose. This hearing is a formal, adversarial proceeding, comparing roughly with a lawsuit in any civil court. The general counsel is represented by a lawyer who presents the case against the respondent, and the respondent is also entitled to be, and usually is, represented by a lawyer. The general counsel has the "burden of proof" in all cases, which means simply that he must establish by reliable and sufficient evidence that an unfair labor practice was committed. The respondent is entitled to present all relevant evidence in his defense to disprove the allegations of the complaint. The charging party may also be represented by separate counsel, who may likewise take part in the hearing and subsequent proceedings.

Some unfair labor practice hearings are extremely dramatic, involving vigorous examination and cross-examination of witnesses, surprise witnesses, and the like. Most hearings, however, are quite businesslike and undramatic, with the parties quietly presenting evidence in a dignified, professional manner. The administrative judge presides over the hearing precisely as a judge presides over any courtroom trial, ruling on disputed items of evidence, maintaining decorum, and keeping the proceedings moving at a reasonable pace. A stenographic reporter takes a verbatim transcript of the hearing, so that each word is preserved for the parties to study and for the Board and courts to review thereafter.

At the end of the hearing, the parties are entitled to file briefs with the administrative judge. In simpler cases, such briefs are unnecessary and may be waived by either or both parties, but in more difficult cases they are common.

When the hearing has concluded and briefs have been filed, the judge begins his study of the record, the briefs, and the

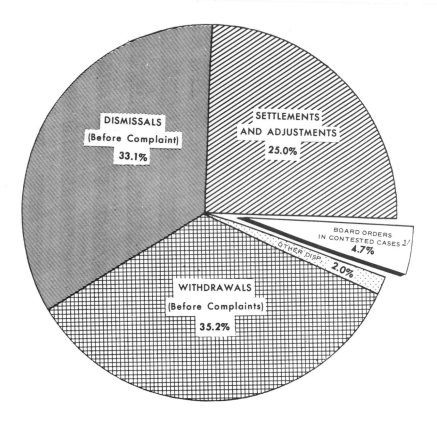

Chart I.
Disposition Pattern for Unfair Labor Practice Cases, Fiscal Year 1972. Based on cases closed.

The volume of unfair labor practice cases processed and the speed with which they are closed as detailed in the above chart are shown in the following table.

Disposition	Number of Cases	Median Days Elapsed
Dismissed before complaint	6,091 (no appeal)	50 (no appeal)
	2,435 (after appeal)	82 (after appeal)
Withdrawn before complaint	8,994	26
Settled and adjusted	4,684 (before complaint)	34 (before complaint)
	1,626 (after complaint)	not available (after complaint)
Contested Board orders	1,199	316

[1] Contested cases reaching Board members for decisions.

applicable law. His work, like that of any other trial judge in this respect, is a lonely, private, and reflective effort to arrive at a decision that bares the truth of the circumstances and that conscientiously applies the Act as written by Congress and interpreted by the Board and courts.

The administrative judge completes his work by writing a formal Decision and Recommendations. This document summarizes the issues, states the facts as the judge finds them, discusses applicable provisions of the statute and precedents, and then determines that the Act has or has not been violated. If he concludes that the respondent has violated the law in one or more respects, the judge will recommend a suitable remedy. His decision, however, is not binding on the general counsel or on the respondent. Any party may file "exceptions" to the judge's findings with the Board in Washington, D.C. In about one-third of the cases, the parties accept the judge's recommendations and do not appeal to the Board. Thus, if the judge recommends that the complaint be dismissed because the evidence fails to prove a violation of the law, the general counsel frequently accepts that result without appealing to the Board. Similarly, in cases where the judge has determined that an employer or labor organization has violated the law, it is common for the respondent to accept that finding and to comply with the recommended remedy. The Act guarantees the right of the respondent, the charging party, and the general counsel to appeal the judge's findings to the Board, however, and this right is frequently exercised, particularly in difficult or important cases.

An appeal to the Board is a relatively simple procedural matter. The appealing party sets forth exceptions to particular findings in the judge's decision, usually accompanying such exceptions with a legal brief. The opposing party may also file a brief in support of the judge's decision. Commonly, a party will appeal from that part of the judge's decision that is adverse to him, while arguing in support of that part of the decision in his favor.

When a case reaches the Board on appeal from an administrative judge's decision, the executive secretary assigns it to one Board member, who, in turn, assigns it to a legal assistant for primary research and analysis. The internal processing of a case thereafter depends on its nature.

Each Board member is the chairman of a panel of three Board members, and all cases begin as panel cases. The vast majority of cases are initially reviewed by a so-called subpanel, consisting of experienced representatives of the three panel members. After meeting with the legal assistant who studied the record and his supervisor, the subpanel makes a tentative decision for disposition of the case; the three Board members of the panel then personally review the tentative disposition before it becomes final. The Board's decision in such cases often takes the form of a "short form adoption," meaning that the Board's official decision is in the nature of a very brief, formal document agreeing with the administrative judge's decision and adopting it in full.

More difficult cases may be referred by the subpanel to their panel of three Board members. A memorandum of the issues presented is then prepared, and the three members then decide the case based on their review of the record and briefs.

Proposed panel decisions are circulated also to nonparticipating Board members for clearance as an extra safeguard for uniformity in the Board's application of the statute.

The most difficult cases are referred either by the subpanel or the panel to the full Board of five members, who usually meet on Tuesday and Friday mornings, accompanied by their respective chief counsel, the executive secretary, and the solicitor. To assist their deliberations, the legal assistant who first studied the case, one from the staff of the Board member to whom the case was assigned, will present a detailed memorandum discussing the important factual and legal aspects of the case. This memorandum normally contains no recommendations but sets forth the major questions and their implications.

In recent years, the Board has also adopted the practice of holding oral arguments in selected, unusually important cases one day each month. These arguments are given before the full Board, prior to the Board's consideration, and are similar to arguments before appellate courts. Counsel for the parties make brief oral statements in support of their positions, and the members of the Board press them with questions.

At the Tuesday and Friday morning conferences of the full Board, discussion among the members and their chief counsel is usually lively and occasionally heated. Some members enter these conferences with firm opinions about how particular cases should be decided. Others will not have made up their minds and will be open to persuasion. It is here, perhaps more vividly than on any other occasion, that the personalities and philosophies of Board members are most fully revealed.

After each member has had the opportunity to express his views concerning the disposition of a case, the Chairman asks each member to cast a tentative vote. If there is a clear majority, those who constitute the majority will instruct the legal assistant to whom the case has been assigned to draft a decision for the Board's consideration. Members who disagree with the majority point of view will have a legal assistant on their staff prepare a dissenting opinion. Thereafter, the majority and minority opinions are circulated to each member for review. Occasionally, a minority member will be persuaded by the majority's draft opinion and vice versa. It is much more common, however, for Board members to stick by their original views, although the majority and minority opinions may be rewritten a number of times to deal with arguments raised by the other side.

The Board decision itself is similar to any appellate court decision, that is, it recites the salient facts, summarizes the parties' main contentions, and then draws conclusions of fact and law. Where the Board finds no violation of the Act, it dismisses the complaint. Where a violation is found, the Board fashions a suitable remedial order.

In one important respect, the Board's decision differs from that of an appellate court: The Board's decision is an institutional product that does not identify the author of the decision, whereas appellate court decisions almost always identify their judicial authors. Of course, the first drafts of most Board decisions are written not by Board members themselves but by one or more of their legal assistants. Still, Board members often write major sections of their own opinions, and some scholars believe it is unfortunate that even the best and most important majority Board decisions are anonymously authored.*

On receipt of the Board's decision, any *aggrieved* party may appeal to a federal court of appeals. A party is aggrieved whenever the Board finds that he has committed an unfair labor practice; similarly, a charging party or a party who has intervened in the case may be aggrieved, if the Board refuses to find an unfair labor practice against the respondent or declines to grant the requested remedy. The appeal is normally taken to the court of appeals for the judicial circuit in which the case arose, the circuit where the aggrieved party resides or does business, or the court of appeals for the District of Columbia circuit—the statute permits this choice. The general counsel who prosecuted the case before the administrative law judge may not appeal against a Board decision, however, even though he is independent of the Board. Once the Board has issued its final decision in an unfair labor practice proceeding, the general counsel changes hats: He is no longer the investigator and prosecutor; he is the Board's lawyer who must defend the Board's decision—whether or not he had sought that decision earlier—in the appellate courts.

---

* If only one Board member dissents from a majority decision, he is obviously the author of his own dissent; if two members dissent, however, there is no way for an outsider to know which of them authored the dissent.

An extraordinarily large number of the Board's unfair labor practice decisions are appealed each year to the federal appellate courts. The relations between the courts and the Board will be discussed in detail in Chapter VI.

Those parties who choose not to appeal the Board's decision have two choices: They may either comply with that decision; or, if they have been found by the Board to have violated the Labor Act, they may simply wait for the Board, by a similar petition in the appropriate circuit, to seek enforcement of its order in the courts.

Following a Board decision in which a party has been ordered to cease an unfair labor practice, further investigations or hearings may be required to determine whether there has been compliance or to determine the amount of back pay to which employees may be entitled under a Board order. On rare occasions, following judicial enforcement of a Board order, contempt proceedings must be initiated against parties who have failed to comply with the court's orders. Parties who are found guilty of contempt are subject to civil and criminal fines.

PROCEDURES IN ELECTION CASES

The NLRB conducts three main kinds of secret-ballot elections: *representation elections,* in which a labor organization seeks to become the exclusive bargaining agent of employees; *decertification elections,* in which employees may decide whether or not they wish to deprive their current bargaining agent of exclusive representation rights; and *deauthorization elections,* in which employees may decide whether they wish to deprive their current bargaining agent of authority to enter into union shop arrangements with their employer.

Who may seek an NLRB election, *how* to secure an election, and *when* an election may be conducted are also complex issues. At the risk of oversimplification, the general answers to these questions are as follows:

Who May Seek an NLRB Election?

Depending on the circumstances, employees, a labor organization, an individual, or an employer may petition the NLRB to conduct an election. The most familiar election is the representation election sought by a labor organization. The Labor Act permits individuals to serve as the exclusive bargaining agent for employees, and there have been a very few instances in which individuals have petitioned the Board. The Act also authorizes an employee or group of employees to petition for an election to certify a bargaining agent independently of a labor organization, but this rarely—if ever— has occurred.

The Taft-Hartley Act allows employers to file an election petition, if they have received a demand for recognition from a labor organization or individual. Otherwise, employers may not initiate election proceedings.

Individuals, employees, or labor organizations may file decertification election petitions, but employees and only employees may file union shop de-authorization election petitions.

How Does One Secure an NLRB Election?

Conducting secret-ballot elections is both expensive to the government and a source of uncertainty in the workplace. Thus, in the combined interest of economy and stability of labor relations, the Act establishes minimum conditions that must be satisfied in order to start the Board's election machinery. The most important of these is called the "showing of interest."

When a union seeks a representation election, it must show by reliable proof, the Board holds, that no fewer than 30 per cent of the employees in an appropriate bargaining unit wish that union to represent them for purposes of collective bargaining; that is the showing of interest required. Usually, a union makes such a showing by presenting signed authorization cards or employee petitions. If a labor organization cannot garner this minimum support from employees, the Act assumes that it would be futile to conduct an election.

Similarly, when employees seek a decertification or union shop de-authorization election, they, too, must make such a 30 per cent showing of interest.

The only exception to this rule applies to employers, who are entitled to file an election petition whenever a union demands recognition from them. Under recent Board decisions, however, the employer who files a representation petition must produce a minimal amount of evidence that his employees are dissatisfied with their *current* bargaining agent before the employer can require such an incumbent union to submit to an election.

When Will an NLRB Election Be Conducted?

The Board does not conduct elections whenever a petition is filed. The petition must be "timely," and timeliness is a complex concept in relation to NLRB elections.

The NLRB is barred by the statute, for example, from conducting more than one election in a bargaining unit during any 12-month period. Again, the policy underlying this 12-month rule is that elections are both expensive and disruptive; hence, Congress believed that they should be conducted no more often than once each year in any bargaining unit.

In addition to the 12-month rule, the Board has developed a series of "contract bar" rules. These are designed to provide stability in situations where a collective bargaining agreement is in effect *and* at the same time to permit employees free choice of bargaining agents. These dual objectives are achieved by the basic contract bar rule that no election will be conducted during the first three years of any contract that has a term of more than three years. And, of course, no election will normally be conducted during the life of a collective bargaining agreement whose term is less than three years.

This 3-year bar rule has changed over the years. In the earliest days of the Wagner Act, the bar period was rarely more than one year, although it was officially stated as a "reasonable" period of time. Little by little, the Board has lengthened the period in response to the industry practice of negotiating long-term contracts.

There are a number of other rules related to the contract bar doctrine, and they, too, have often been modified. Although space does not permit a full exploration of the various contract bar rules and exceptions to these rules, they have received almost universal approval from labor and management as clear and predictable guides to the parties.

If an election petition meets these preliminary standards— it is filed by a suitable party, supported by an adequate "showing of interest," and is timely—the election procedures of the Act become operative.

Elections are conducted by the Board only in "units appropriate for collective bargaining." Thus, the final hurdle in the path of the party seeking an election is proof that he seeks an election in such an *appropriate unit*. In Chapter VII we shall discuss in detail the importance of unit policies. Here it is simply important to note that unit issues are often very controversial: Unions always seek election units in which their chances of winning are best; similarly, employers seek election units in which their best interests are most likely to be realized. This collision of interests often leads to litigation in which the Board is required to determine the unit.

In a remarkably high percentage of cases, the parties themselves reach agreement on the unit in which an election should be conducted. Provided that the agreement is consistent with NLRB unit policies, the Board will normally respect the decision and conduct an election in that unit. When the parties agree between themselves on a unit, it is possible to conduct the election within a short time after the election petition has been filed.

Each year 75–80 per cent of the agency's 9,000 representation elections are conducted under such consent agreements. This reflects the rather general understanding and acceptance of the Board's election rules and the skill of its regional staff in bringing opposing parties together within the framework of those rules.

When the parties disagree as to the unit or another relevant issue, the Board, acting through its regional directors, will direct that a hearing, conducted by hearing officers (attorneys or field examiners) be held. A representation hearing is an investigation of the facts surrounding the petition and is, at least in theory, less formal and legalistic than an unfair labor practice hearing. Nonetheless, because of the importance of the representation hearing to both parties, they are often represented by counsel, and the hearing is frequently a hard-fought legal contest.

At the representation hearing, the parties present evidence concerning the appropriate geographic scope of the unit, the supervisory status of individuals, the eligibility of other persons such as guards and confidential employees, contract bar issues, and other such matters. Again, as in unfair labor practice hearings, a stenographic reporter transcribes the proceeding verbatim. Following the hearing each party is entitled to file briefs with the regional director or with the Board if the regional director has sent the case there for decision.

Since 1961, when the NLRB invoked its authority under the Landrum-Griffin Amendments to delegate power to decide unit and other representation case issues, the vast majority of contested cases has been decided by the thirty-one regional directors. Only in an unusually important or novel case will the regional director transfer the proceeding to the NLRB in Washington for decision. The two parties accept the decision of the regional director in about three out of four cases, but the parties are entitled to request a Board review of his determination of the issues on a limited number of grounds: The regional director has departed from Board precedents; the case raises an important, unresolved question of law or policy; the regional director's decision contains important factual errors; the conduct of the hearing was improper in some major respect; or the decision raises questions of existing Board policy that the Board should reconsider.

Although the Board carefully considers all requests for review of regional directors' determinations, it grants them only rarely. When such a request is received by the Board, it is assigned for study to one of a special group of NLRB attorneys who work only on representation cases. They evaluate the merits of the review request and present recommendations for its disposition to a subpanel presided over by a single member of the Board who has been designated "member of the month." He decides whether or not to recommend the grant of the request, in conjunction with representatives of other Board panel members in routine cases or in personal conference with Board members in more difficult ones. In all cases the Board panel members approve the tentative decision before it becomes final.

Of course, the regional director or the Board will not direct an election in every case. If the petitioner has sought an election in a unit inappropriate for bargaining, the regional director or the Board will dismiss the petition. On the other hand, if the requested unit is not significantly different from the unit that the regional director or the Board ultimately determines to be appropriate, an election will be directed in the latter unit. For example, if the petitioning union seeks an election in only one department in a multidepartment plant, and the regional director determines that a single-department unit is not appropriate, the election petition would be dismissed because the appropriate and inappropriate units are significantly different. Moreover, the union's showing of interest in the single-department unit would be insufficient to justify an election in the larger unit. However, a petition will

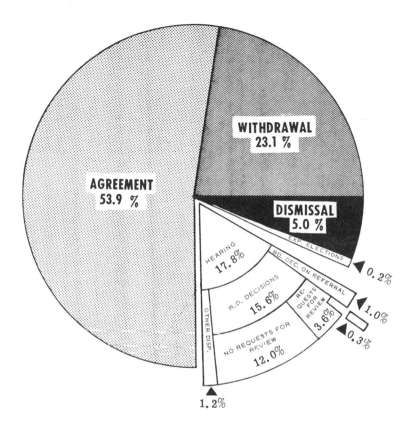

Chart II.
DISPOSITION PATTERN FOR REPRESENTATION CASES, FISCAL
YEAR 1972. Based on cases closed.

The following table shows the number of representation cases processed
and the time within which they are closed as detailed in the above chart.

Disposition	Number of Cases	Median Days Elapsed
Elections under agreements	7,246	52
Withdrawals	3,097	22
Dismissals	678	39
Regional directors' decisions	2,052	47 (filing to decision)
Board decisions on referral	129	237

* These cases also counted under Regional Director's Decisions.

not normally be dismissed because the petitioning union improperly sought to include a number of persons whom the regional director finds are "supervisors" and must be excluded.

Once an election has been directed—whether by the Board itself, or, more commonly, by a regional director—notices will be sent to the employer and must be prominently posted to inform employees about the time and the place of the election and the eligibility of voters.

Since 1966, when an election has been directed, the employer has also been required to furnish a list with the names and addresses of all employees in the bargaining unit for the use of all parties. This improves the opportunity to have an informed electorate and facilitates the testing of voter eligibility.

NLRB elections are normally conducted during working hours on the employer's premises. An agent of the regional office directs the election, taking every reasonable precaution to assure the integrity of the secret-ballot process. Each party to the election is entitled to have at least one observer at the polling place, who may challenge any prospective voter on the ground that he is not eligible to vote under the Board's unit determination. When such a person is challenged, his vote is set aside in a sealed envelope for later consideration. The Board agent conducting the election is also entitled to challenge voters whose names do not appear on the current payroll that the employer is required to supply the NLRB before the election.

Historically, employees have participated in NLRB elections in large numbers. Rarely do fewer than 90 per cent of eligible voters participate, a far higher rate of participation than is customary in public elections.

When the voting process has been completed, the ballots are counted by the NLRB election agent in the presence of the parties' observers, who are requested to sign an election tally form. If the challenged votes are sufficient to affect the outcome of the election, they must be evaluated and a determination of their validity made by the regional director. Sometimes, if important questions of fact are related to the challenges, he will conduct a hearing on challenged ballots; otherwise, he will simply issue a report making his determination.

A majority of those actually participating in the election—rather than a majority of those eligible to vote—is required in all NLRB elections. Thus, if an election results in a tie vote, a petitioning union does not win, because it lacks a majority.

If two or more labor organizations appear on the ballot and neither of them nor the "no union" choice receives a majority of the ballots, the Board conducts a runoff election between those two choices receiving the largest number of votes. For example, in a representation election with 100 eligible voters, if 40 cast their ballots for Union A, 40 cast ballots for Union B, and 20 cast ballots for the "no union" choice, a runoff election would be conducted between the two unions, eliminating the "no union" choice. However, if Union A received 40 votes, "no union" received 40 votes, and Union B received 20 votes, the runoff election would be conducted between Union A and the "no union" choice, eliminating Union B.

Under the Board's rules and regulations, any party to the election may file "objections" to its conduct with the regional director. So-called objections cases permit the Board to review evidence presented by the parties that the election was interfered with by improper conduct. This is an intricate area of the Board's work, and there are many sharp disagreements over what type of conduct constitutes interference. In general, unfair labor practices committed *after* the filing of an election petition interfere with the election. Other types of conduct, however—not amounting to an unfair labor practice—might also sufficiently interfere with the fairness of an election to warrant setting aside the results. Certain kinds of campaign trickery, misrepresentations, or community-intrusions creating an atmosphere of fear during the campaign might come into this category, even though they might not violate the unfair labor practice provisions of the Labor Act. Literally, any kind of conduct that precludes a fair and free election, including misconduct by the Board's own agents, might be grounds for filing objections, and almost 900 such cases may be decided by the regional director or the Board in a typical year.

If the regional director believes that the objections are substantial, he may direct that a new election be held or that a hearing be conducted to determine the validity of the objections. Depending on the nature of the case, the regional director's decision on objections may be final; in certain cases, however, a losing party may ask the Board in Washington to review the regional director's decision. If the regional director or the Board determines that conduct interfered with the fairness of the election, a new election will be held, and this "rerun" election is precisely like the first one.

The issues raised by challenges to voters are determined by postelection procedures similar to those for objections.

If no objections are filed after an election, or if objections are ultimately dismissed by the regional director or the Board, the NLRB issues a "certification" of the results of the election. When a union has sought representation rights, this certification establishes its legal right to act as the collective bargaining agent of employees and, in effect, establishes the employer's legal duty to engage in bargaining with that union. Similarly, in a decertification election, the issuance of formal certification that the union no longer represents a majority of employees prohibits the union as of that time from acting as the exclusive agent of employees and prohibits the employer from dealing with the union for purposes of collective bargaining.

Although the Board's unfair labor practice decisions may be appealed by any aggrieved party to the federal courts of appeals for review, the Act does *not* permit direct judicial review of election cases. Congress legislated this distinction for good reason: It wished to encourage the parties in election cases to get to the bargaining table quickly and to resolve their disputes without the delay that inevitably accompanies court litigation. Nonetheless, indirect judicial review of the Board's election orders and postelection decisions on objections and challenges is permitted through the complex unfair labor practice route. If, for example, an employer disagrees with a unit determination by the Board and a union wins in the election that follows, the employer may not rush off to court to test the legal validity of the Board's unit decision. He may, however, secure a legal test of that decision by refusing to bargain with the union on the ground that the unit decision was contrary to law. In order to compel the employer to honor its certification and to bargain, the union is very likely to file a refusal-to-bargain charge against the employer. In such circumstances, the general counsel will almost certainly issue a complaint, and the employer may then defend himself on the basis that the unit in which the election was conducted was contrary to law. The Board will not upset its own unit determination in the subsequent unfair labor practice case; on the contrary, it will almost automatically rule that the employer's refusal to bargain in these circumstances is illegal. However, the employer may then seek judicial review of the bargaining order, along with the Board's earlier unit determination. The Act does not afford the same opportunity for court review to unions losing their representation cases before the Board.

Notwithstanding this long and circuitous process for review of the Board's representation case proceedings, the courts accord special respect to the Board's expertise in this area; they, therefore, only rarely upset the Board's election orders.

THE OVERLAP

As might be expected, a large proportion of unfair labor practice cases arise in union-organizing situations. It is at the point of attempted union growth that the conflict tends to be most bitter and unlawful. Consequently, there is an extensive overlap and interaction between the representation and unfair labor practice cases described above. The investigations and the settlement efforts in one context will frequently be useful in the other, and hearings may be consolidated because the issues in both cases are common. The Board's experience thus has demonstrated the wisdom of the congressional decision to lodge in one agency the responsibility for both functions and the folly of proposals to separate them by delegating the unfair practice jurisdiction to courts. The guise of "labor-law reform" cannot conceal the necessarily obstructive effects of such a change.

RULE-MAKING

Some Board watchers over the years—and the Supreme Court in one leading case—have criticized the Board for failing to utilize its authority under Section 6 of the Act to engage in "rule-making," i.e., the promulgation, after public notice in the *Federal Register* and an opportunity to all parties so desiring to present their views, of rules of general future application to give detailed content to the various requirements of the statute. Board members and practitioners, with few exceptions, have considered most issues in unfair labor practice and representation cases not well suited to resolution in this broadside, quasi-legislative manner. Under the pressure of its growing case load, however, the Board, since 1970, has for the first time engaged in rule-making in cases concerning jurisdictional standards, and, with some firm prodding from the courts, especially Judge Henry J. Friendly of the Second Circuit, it is likely to use this procedure more in the future.

VI

The NLRB's Relations with Congress, the President, and the Federal Courts

The federal Constitution provides for only three branches of government: an executive, a judiciary, and a legislature. There is no mention of the independent regulatory agencies that, like the National Labor Relations Board, are not subject to the supervision of the President, the federal courts, or legislative bodies in any conventional sense. What, then, is the status of such independent commissions and agencies as the NLRB, the Federal Trade Commission, the Interstate Commerce Commission, the Securities and Exchange Commission, the Civil Aeronautics Board, the Federal Communications Commission, the Federal Power Commission, and the Atomic Energy Commission? Students of Constitutional and administrative law have tried to determine the answer to this question since the late nineteenth century, when the first independent commission, the Interstate Commerce Commission, was created by Congress.

The NLRB's Status in Our Constitutional System

According to one of the oldest Constitutional theories, these agencies are essentially "arms of Congress." By this reasoning, when Congress enacts a broad, regulatory statute and establishes an independent agency to administer it, Congress has delegated its own legislative powers to the agency to "fill in the gaps" of the legislation. Thus, independent agencies owe their primary loyalty to Congress.

There are competing theories, however. Some students of the field consider regulatory commissions to be extensions of the power of the President. After all, commission members are appointed by him; their budgets are approved by his office; and their work is similar in many ways to Cabinet-level, executive departments that are, of course, directly under his supervision.

Not surprisingly, proponents of a third theory hold that regulatory agencies are primarily judicial bodies—in all but name—because so much of their work involves formal decision-making in the context of adversarial litigation. Indeed, there have been innumerable proposals over the years to convert the NLRB into a federal labor court that would perform virtually the same duties as the Board now does, except that its members would be federal judges with lifetime tenure.

Advocates of a fourth, more contemporary view hold that independent agencies are a "blend" of executive, legislative, and judicial powers. This is the position, for example, of the late Dean James Landis, a leading scholar of administrative law, who commented that regulatory agencies exercise an "assemblage of rights normally exercisable by government as a whole." In the nineteenth century, when the separation-of-powers doctrine was a hotly disputed Constitutional precept, how independent agencies were viewed may have made a difference. Today, however, most Constitutional scholars have rejected the separation-of-powers doctrine in favor of the more flexible concept of checks and balances. Under the checks and balances theory, the rigid separation of the three branches of government is not as important as each branch's having some kind of check on the others' exercise of power and authority.*

RELATIONS WITH CONGRESS

It is difficult to generalize about the NLRB's relations with Congress, except in formal and artificial terms. A realistic understanding of this relationship requires some appreciation for the unwritten, informal dynamics of our national political system. To put it plainly, the most important relations have little public visibility and operate on a highly informal, unstructured basis.

In a purely legal sense, the Board has only three formal and regular contacts with Congress: when the Senate is called on to confirm Presidential nominees to the Board, when the Board's annual appropriation comes before Congress, and when the Board submits its annual report to Congress.

The Confirmation Process

Under the Taft-Hartley Act, each member of the Board is nominated by the President for a normal term of five years, subject to confirmation by the Senate. Similarly, the general counsel is nominated by the President, but for a term of four years. In the Board's entire history, no Presidential nominee for member or general counsel of the Board has ever been denied confirmation by the Senate. This record can be explained less by the qualifications of each nominee than by the fact that the Senate rarely exercises its power to challenge the President's choices for membership on *any* of the federal regulatory agencies. It is no secret, of course, that, in addition to its inquiries in labor-management circles, the White House

---

* The court decisions just preceding the departure of Special Prosecutor Archibald Cox are good examples of this trend.

commonly clears such intended nominees with relevant Senate leaders to forestall or avoid confrontations. The better the "advice," the surer the "consent."

When the President announces his nomination for NLRB membership, it is customary for the nominee to visit the chairman and several ranking senators who sit on the Senate Labor and Public Welfare Committee; these are usually courtesy calls. Thereafter, the committee schedules a formal confirmation hearing, where the nominee is customarily introduced by one senator from his home state. Occasionally, the committee will ask the nominee a few perfunctory questions about his views; more often than not, the committee disposes of the formal hearing process in a few minutes with no questions whatever.

There have been a few instances in which nominees have been closely examined by one or more hostile members of the Senate Labor Committee. The spirited examination in 1965 of one of the co-authors of this book during the two hearings on his nomination for a second term demonstrated how the confirmation process can be utilized in committee to express congressional concern over an agency's substantive decisions. But this is rare. Usually, the committee reports each nominee favorably to the floor of the Senate for confirmation. There, nominations to the Board are generally approved without question, debate, or comment. The case of Albert Beeson, discussed in Chapter III, was the single exception of a nomination that provoked a serious Senate debate and a narrow vote of approval.

Some Senate observers argue that it has failed to satisfy its Constitutional obligation to scrutinize Presidential appointees to the NLRB as well as to hundreds of other major government posts. But the growth of the federal bureaucracy makes it difficult for the Senate to give close consideration to any but the very highest government posts. Given the prior clearance of nominees with congressional leaders, moreover, the strong tradition of respect accorded to the President's wishes makes it unlikely that the Senate will often use the confirmation process as an opportunity to examine the work of the Board or other agencies.

The Appropriation Process

The Board's annual budget in recent years has been over $50 million. Each fiscal year the NLRB must submit its budget requests both to a House and a Senate appropriations subcommittee; prior to this request, however, the Board's budget must be scrutinized and approved by the Office of Management and Budget.

The NLRB's relatively small budget—a fraction of the cost of a single moon landing—is supported before the appropriations subcommittees with graphic and statistical evidence of the agency's needs. Usually, its budget is routinely approved by Congress. NLRB funds, however, are considered by Congress with a multi-agency group that includes the Department of Labor and the Department of Health, Education, and Welfare. Because the annual appropriations for these departments, especially HEW, are often controversial, the Board's appropriation has occasionally been delayed and jeopardized.

The agency's money needs are based on expected work load. They, therefore, rest wholly on estimates of how many unfair labor practice charges and representation petitions will be filed by private parties in the year to follow and on the nature of the agency investigation, settlement, and litigation work that will be required to dispose of them. The care, not to say caution, with which these educated guesses are made has, over the years, had two results: First, the estimates have proven to be remarkably accurate; second, the congressional appropriations committees and their inquiring staffs have developed a high degree of confidence in the reliability of these budget figures, although committee members often ask probing questions to test the Board's justifications. Over the past eleven years, final appropriations have almost exactly matched appropriations requests, and, thus, the agency's fiscal-credibility rating in Congress in recent years has been high.

Occasionally, the appropriations hearing will be utilized for review of some phase of the agency work to which a committee member has been alerted.

The Annual Report

The Taft-Hartley Act requires the Board to submit an annual report of its activities to Congress and the President. This formal report is routinely filed each year and is rarely the subject of any official attention. In addition, the agency prepares and publishes for Congress, the labor-management community, and the public a more comprehensive report, summarizing and interpreting the year's work, the leading cases, novel and significant applications of the law by the Board and courts, and basic trends in the administration of the law as reflected in statistical analyses. These annual reports are invaluable research guides to scholars and other NLRB observers.

Besides these three formal and regular points of contact between Congress and the Board, there are many other more informal relations. The most important of these is undoubtedly the "oversight" hearing by a committee of either the Senate or House. Other kinds of congressional hearings, however, occasionally involve the Board as well.

The Oversight Hearing

An oversight hearing is one in which an appropriate congressional committee, acting under the authority given to it by the Legislative Reorganization Act of 1946, *oversees* or reviews the work of an agency. The NLRB's oversight or parent committees are the Senate and House Labor committees. In the last two decades, these committees have been so busy with more pressing affairs that, for better or worse, they have seldom surveyed the Board. (The Board prefers to say that it has performed its duties with such fidelity to Congress's purposes that there has been no need for regular oversight hearings.) Needless to say, this matter is deeply enmeshed with national politics, in the sense that congressional committees do not spend their valuable time performing the routine maintenance of finding out what small federal agencies have been up to, unless the agency is doing something very controversial or for some reason otherwise displeases its oversight committee—or those who have its ear.

There have been periodic hearings on the Board's work over the years. A few were unmistakably encouraged by the desires and asserted grievances of interested labor or management parties. The 1961 hearings of the Pucinski subcommittee on the NLRB, for example, were mainly an assault by prolabor spokesmen on what they perceived as the promanagement, Eisenhower NLRB of the 1950's. Similarly, the Ervin subcommittee hearings of 1968 were an attack by promanagement representatives on what they saw as the prolabor, Kennedy-Johnson NLRB of the 1960's.

Since 1939, when the extremely conservative Smith committee investigated the NLRB, there have been a number of such blatantly partisan, one-sided hearings. These do not qualify as legitimate oversight hearings. They are prompted by interested parties hoping to influence Congress either to amend the law or urge the Board to modify its interpretation of it. Obviously, these parties hope that the Board, looking over its shoulder, will decide future cases with more circumspection. This kind of hearing is hardly a disinterested exercise in discovering the most reasonable or effective way to carry out the purpose of the law. Even so, when the partisan chaff is blown away, such hearings and the reports that result from them can be useful vehicles for criticism, gauges of the law's effectiveness, and shocking reminders of the bitter cleavage that still divides labor and management.

Unfortunately, congressional committees rarely have the time or inclination to engage in periodic, objective studies of the work of federal agencies to determine whether the federal law is being administered wisely and efficiently.

Substantive Hearings

It is customary to invite the Chairman of the NLRB to testify when a subcommittee of the House or Senate Labor Committee conducts hearings on proposed amendments to the Labor Act. In recent years, the Board has, for the most part, carefully refrained from expressing any opinion on the merits of pending legislation, so that the Board is not put in the position of prejudging the merits of a law that it may later be called on to enforce. The Board willingly testifies, however, on amendments that affect the Board's own procedures. And, of course, the Board usually is willing to extend full cooperation to any congressional committee that requests objective information or studies.

Other Formal and Informal Contacts with Congress

Almost daily, the NLRB receives letters from members of Congress, on behalf of constituents, inquiring about the status of cases pending before the Board. These letters of inquiry are normally quite proper; they merely ask, as any citizen or litigant is entitled to do, when the Board will issue its decision in a pending case, and they are answered with the most reliable information the Board has.

RELATIONS WITH THE PRESIDENT

The NLRB's relations with the White House are relatively formal and fall into three main categories: appointments, appropriations, and information.

Appointments

The White House's primary influence on the Board, as well as on the courts and all other agencies, derives from the appointment process. Once a Presidential nominee to the NLRB has been confirmed by the Senate, however, the White House's influence over the appointee's official performance of his duties theoretically comes to an end.

One of the fascinating and largely unstudied questions about the NLRB is how the White House makes nominations. The post is not a plum sought by large campaign contributors; there is too much work. The necessities of decision-making expose the incumbent to constant cross fire, and the job is not a natural springboard to higher preferments. Many individuals are reluctant to leave important private positions for the slings and arrows of this particular public service. The very least that can be said is that, even if it tried, the White House could seldom hope to secure the persons best qualified by training, experience, and temperament to serve on the Board.

There have been many highly qualified and distinguished appointments during the Board's long history, but all appointments to the Board have been "political," in both the best and worst senses of the word. Rarely does the White House nominate a candidate whose over-all political and philosophical orientation is hostile to the President's. Robert Denham's appointment as the Board's first general counsel in 1947 was such a rare instance, and, as indicated in earlier chapters, that appointment was the source of great difficulty for the White House and the Board itself.

On the other hand, the White House normally—but not always—is careful to determine that its nominees to the Board are, at least, acceptable both to the labor and management communities. In fact, both sides are informally contacted by the White House, usually through the Secretary of Labor, before appointments are publicly announced. This informal preappointment communication assures the President that his nominees will not meet with extreme opposition during the confirmation hearings.

In the hierarchy of the federal establishment, the Board is relatively low in importance to the White House, by comparison with members of the President's Cabinet, for example. Thus, although it is customary for the President to meet briefly with a nominee before a formal announcement of his appointment is released, this meeting is largely ceremonial and perfunctory; and the President is not likely to have any personal knowledge of his appointees to the Board.

Appropriations

The Board's annual appropriation is based on a budget prepared by the agency and closely reviewed and approved by the White House's Office of Management and the Budget. In this sense, the President has "power of the purse strings" over the Board; but this power, although exercised with great diligence, is never used to control the agency's substantive work.

Unlike work flow in Cabinet-level departments and other "program" agencies—such as the Department of Labor—the Board's cannot be determined by the agency itself. The Board has no control over the number of election petitions and unfair labor practice charges that are filed with it during any fiscal year. Thus, its budgetary requirements are rather inflexible.

Information

The White House occasionally consults the Board, through the Secretary of Labor, about a variety of labor-relations issues. For example, in the late 1960's, the Chairman of the Board served on a task force that studied the operation of President Kennedy's Executive Order 10988, governing labor relations between federal agencies and federal employee organizations.

The White House occasionally receives letters from citizens inquiring about the work of the Board or about particular cases pending before the Board. These letters are sent to the Board with a request either that the Board answer the inquiry directly or that it prepare a proposed answer to be sent by the White House. Like congressional inquiries, those from the White House are perfectly proper and routine. They never seek to influence the outcome of a pending case; they merely seek legitimate information about the status of a case. The Board answers such letters precisely as it would answer similar letters sent directly to it.

The Secretary of Labor is the White House's principal liaison with the NLRB with respect to all matters of public policy. In every administration, however, the President also assigns responsibility for liaison with the independent regulatory agencies to a member of the White House staff, usually a special assistant to the President. Because it is universally recognized that the independent agencies perform judicial functions, and, therefore, that it is improper for the White House or anyone else to discuss pending cases with the Board *ex parte,* the White House historically has been scrupulously careful not to contact the NLRB about the merits of pending cases.

From time to time, the White House has attempted to shape the philosophical direction of the Board through the appointment process, but it has never been suggested that the White House attempted to influence the outcome of particular cases. Whether individual Board members are conscious of White House politics when they decide cases is a very different —and very private—matter.

Other Executive Agencies

Obviously, the NLRB cannot always act in splendid isolation. When other federal agencies are involved in situations brought to the Board by an election petition or unfair practice charge, there is candid and continuous exchange of information. This is particularly true in the case of the Federal Mediation and Conciliation Service (FMCS), where strikes or strike threats with which the service is dealing may have an impact on the NLRB's action, and vice versa. The Board also advises the FMCS of all certifications of union representatives in Board elections. This enables the service to be ready to assist the employer and the union, if needed, to achieve a successful resolution of differences in their first experience with collective bargaining. Where there is a similar overlap with other agencies in the labor-relations field, communication is essential.

RELATIONS WITH THE FEDERAL COURTS

Any party who has been aggrieved by an unfair labor practice decision of the Board may appeal to the federal circuit courts of appeals. And, because the Board's orders are not self-enforcing, the Board itself must present its orders for enforcement to a court of appeals. As a result, the Board has an immense volume of litigation in the appellate courts. In recent years, more than half of all unfair labor practice decisions of the Board have been appealed by one party or have been taken to an appellate court by the Board to seek enforcement. As a practical matter this means that each year approximately 350 to 400 new NLRB cases end up in the courts of appeals.

Not only does the NLRB have far more appellate cases than any other federal board or commission, its cases constitute nearly half of *all* appellate cases involving federal boards and commissions. The explanation for this phenomenon is that the NLRB decides far more cases that are *subject* to judicial review than any other federal agency.

The Board fares well in the courts of appeals: Although the statistics vary slightly from year to year, in the average year the Board's decisions are upheld by the courts in approximately 85 per cent of all cases. This figure is somewhat misleading, however, because roughly 20 per cent of these cases involve *some* modification of the Board's order.

Many cases that are decided in the Board's favor by the courts of appeals are the subject of petitions for *certiorari* in the Supreme Court. Of these, the Supreme Court grants only a tiny fraction and reviews a handful of cases, in which the NLRB is a party, involving the interpretation of the Labor Act. These are the most important cases, deciding previously unresolved issues of broad applicability to the labor-management community.

Perhaps no area of the Board's work has been more carefully studied than judicial reaction to NLRB decisions. Most labor-law scholars specialize in analysis of judicial decisions that deal with major interpretations of the Labor Act. In addition to a vast literature of law review articles dealing with judicial views on substantive issues, a growing body of periodical literature assesses how the federal courts *perceive* the NLRB's work. For example, scholars have studied whether particular courts have confidence in the Board's findings of fact in various types of cases and have examined how much "deference" or respect the courts grant to the Board's primary interpretation of the Act.

Because more than half of all NLRB unfair labor practice decisions are reviewed in the courts each year, it is evident that the courts play an extraordinarily important role in the ultimate administration of the Act. Virtually every Board decision is either guided by prior judicial precedents or subject to judicial review. In this sense, the federal judiciary is deeply involved in the Board's daily work, more so perhaps than with any other agency. The ubiquity of the federal judicial system in the administration of the Labor Act is a matter of concern to persons who have studied the operations of the Board.

No responsible observer of the Board's work doubts the validity and necessity for judicial review of the Board's decisions in general. The 1947 amendments to the Act, as interpreted by the Supreme Court, made clear Congress's intent that the courts should more actively review the Board's findings and conclusions and not rubber-stamp them. But there is sharp disagreement among scholars and practitioners over *how much* judicial review is desirable in the public interest. One focal point of this controversy concerns the inevitable delay in the enforcement of Board decisions resulting from judicial review. When a party appeals a decision to the appellate courts or when the Board has to seek enforcement of its decision in the courts, the final disposition of that case may be delayed by as much as a year or more. That means, in practical terms, that an employee who has been discharged illegally, for example, must wait for an additional year *after* the Board's decision in his favor before he is entitled to reinstatement in his former job and to back pay. If the discharged employee has been unable to secure other employment during this period, his situation might be desperate. The impact of such delay on others who contemplate exercising their "protected" rights is obvious.

No one seriously suggests that there should be no judicial review of Board decisions involving important questions of statutory interpretation. But many objective persons believe it is unsound public policy to permit parties to have full judicial review of every routine case decided by the Board. Not only does this practice delay, and thereby weaken, the over-all administration of the Act, it also places an oppressive burden on the federal appellate courts. Judge Henry Friendly is one of a number of commentators to advocate making the NLRB's orders self-enforcing, subject to a party's right to file a very prompt appeal with an appellate court. Lightening the burden of the courts to review NLRB decisions will require a combination of greater skill and care on the Board's part in making and justifying its decisions, a wider acceptance by the parties of the purposes of the Act, and more restraint by the courts in intervening in routine, factual-issue cases.

In addition to litigation in the federal appellate courts, which review NLRB decisions directly, the Board has some litigation on the trial level in federal district courts. The Labor Act requires the Board to seek injunctions in these courts when it believes that certain unfair labor practices have occurred involving secondary boycotts, jurisdictional disputes, organization and recognition picketing, and "hot cargo" agreements. The Board's obligation to seek such injunctions—which are designed to preserve the status quo, thereby protecting the charging party, pending the Board's formal unfair labor practice determination—is spelled out in Section 10(1) of the Act. This litigation is quite routine in a legal sense, but it achieves extraordinarily swift relief each year for literally hundreds of employers beleaguered by secondary boycotts and jurisdictional disputes.

Under Section 10(j) of the Act, the Board has broad discretion to seek injunctions in other unfair labor practice cases. In practice, the Board uses its power under this section rarely, scarcely more often than a score of times a year, and in about half of those cases to halt picket-line violence and illegal strikes. Many observers believe the Board's reluctance to use its Section 10(j) discretion more frequently and systematically is unfortunate, for this is one effective way to protect employees from personal hardship, while discriminatory discharge cases that often drag on for years are pending.

Contempt proceedings, against respondents who repeat their violations of the law in the face of court orders, and subpoena enforcement actions round out the list of the agency's principal court litigation.

Finally, the Board, on rare occasions, intervenes in litigation in the state courts. However, it does so only when necessary to protect the Board's jurisdiction from improper interference by the state.

As the foregoing discussion suggests, the courts have a profound influence on virtually every aspect of the Board's work. For this reason, the NLRB has long been a "lawyer's agency."

In many other independent regulatory agencies, economists, statisticians, accountants, and other professionals perform major roles. At the NLRB, however, where the work requires legal training to understand and anticipate judicial reactions, lawyers are the main group of professionals employed. Others with industrial-relations training perform important tasks as field examiners in the regional offices.

RELATIONS WITH THE LABOR-MANAGEMENT COMMUNITY

Through participation by Board members and the general counsel in a variety of conferences, conventions, and meetings, the agency maintains good relations with major organizations in the labor-relations field. The Board keeps a close liaison, for example, with the Labor Relations Law Section of the American Bar Association and with the National Academy of Arbitrators. Officials of the NLRB are frequently invited to speak before labor and management groups, as well as before college and university audiences, to review and comment on major Board and court decisions. These communications serve the valuable purpose of giving broad notice of the agency's work to employers and unions alike and simultaneously of keeping the agency abreast of public reactions.

VII

Secret-Ballot Elections on the Job

"Industrial democracy" is an old phrase that means many things to many people. From the earliest days of the Industrial Revolution, industrial democracy has been an *ideal* of workers, owners, political reformers, philosophers, and politicians. As early as 1797, Albert Gallatin, who served as Secretary of the Treasury under Jefferson and Madison, said, "The democratic principle on which this nation was founded should not be restricted to the political process but should be applied to the industrial operation as well."

Although the ideal of industrial democracy has been given a great variety of meanings, two dominant ones have survived in the twentieth century: To Marxists, industrial democracy means public ownership of productive enterprises on the socialist model. To non-Marxists, the phrase denotes recognition of the legitimacy of labor unions and the institution of collective bargaining.

The Wagner Act, born in an era of unprecedented industrial turbulence, firmly adopted the nonsocialist alternative for the United States. For the first time in the nation's history, a clear concept of industrial democracy was declared by the Congress to be implemented and guaranteed through National Labor Relations Board elections.

The Significance of NLRB Elections

Management strongly resisted the very idea of elections conducted by the federal government, for elections inevitably meant that management authority over workers was not absolute. Elections symbolized the right of workers to participate in the process of deciding the rules and conditions that would govern their employment, and management feared having to share its traditional authority in the workplace. Even some unions, unsure whether they truly enjoyed the support of the employees whom they represented, were deeply apprehensive about workers' elections, and well they might have been. NLRB elections *have* required management to share some authority over the working lives of employees; and some unions *have* been displaced, because they did not truly represent the wishes of workers.

But these fears of the mid-1930's have long since dissipated. Today the secret-ballot election has become the rare subject on which labor and management agree with enthusiasm.

In 1967, the National Labor Relations Board organized a celebration in honor of a remarkable occasion. On March 2 of that year, Leonard P. Scheno, an employee of the Reynolds Metals Company, cast the twenty-five-millionth vote in NLRB elections. After 25 million NLRB ballots had been cast, labor and management spokesmen outdid each other in eloquent praise for secret-ballot elections.

William F. May, Chairman of the Industrial Relations Committee of the National Association of Manufacturers, said:

> We place a high value in this country on the right of self-determination, whether it be to vote freely for government representatives or, in this case, to vote on whether to have a bargaining representative. We recognize that the expression of individual freedom is a vital aspect of the dignity of man. . . .
> The same democratic principles which inspired the secret ballot election have produced free collective bargaining. . . .
> Despite occasional breakdowns, the collective bargaining proc-

ess has been an important stabilizing influence in our industrial system, and we take this opportunity to reaffirm the need to preserve rather than destroy it.

Few corporate leaders would disagree with Mr. May today, whatever they may have thought in 1935. Their attitude has changed not so much because the business community is less fearful of unions and collective bargaining but because secret-ballot elections have been a brilliant success. From management's point of view, the election system has virtually eliminated a struggle over union recognition rights as a prolific source of strikes and has also eliminated much conflict between rival unions. From labor's point of view, the NLRB election symbolizes society's acceptance of the legitimacy of workers' organizations and freedom of choice on the job. From the individual worker's point of view, the secret ballot guarantees that he may choose whether or not to engage in collective bargaining at all and, if so, which labor organization he wishes as his bargaining agent. Most important, from the public's point of view, the NLRB election has become a fair and orderly institution for the resolution of dangerous and unproductive labor disputes over representation issues in industry.

Although hundreds of bills have been introduced to amend the Labor Act over the years, none within recent memory has proposed elimination of the secret-ballot election.

Testifying before the La Follette committee in 1937, Philip Murray of the Steel Workers Organizing Committee described how the Board's election machinery facilitated resolution of a strike by 25,000 workers of the Jones & Laughlin Steel Corporation in Aliquippa and Pittsburgh in the spring of that year:

> Happily for the workers and the corporation, the National Labor Relations Board was in existence. Because of the existence of the Board, the Jones & Laughlin strike was one of the shortest on record, involving approximately 25,000 workers. It lasted just thirty-six hours.

In the past there would have been no other way out than a long-drawn-out battle, but here under the Wagner Act there was a definite, sane, constitutional and democratic way of settling our differences. The company said we did not really represent its men. SWOC insisted that it did. The obvious way to settle it, therefore, was to hold an election.

The National Labor Relations Board provided the machinery for this, and the strike was settled with an agreement that the terms of the U.S. Steel contract would be in effect until an election was held by the National Labor Relations Board within 10 days to determine whether or not the Steel Workers Organizing Committee represented a majority of the Jones & Laughlin employees. The result was a smashing victory—17,208 for the union and 7,207 against the union.

The Jones & Laughlin Corporation thereupon signed a collective bargaining contract with the SWOC, recognizing it as the sole bargaining agency for all of its production and maintenance workers. This contract was the beginning of the extension of democratic principles and procedures into the operation of the Jones & Laughlin works. . . . Here was an overt experiment in democratic ways. . . .

The Jones & Laughlin election was one of the largest conducted by the National Labor Relations Board. It represents a great victory of reason over strife in American industrial life.

Most NLRB elections today are routinely conducted, lacking in outward drama. But in the early years of the Labor Act, these elections resulted in dramatic confrontations. In the rural South, black workers who had been dissuaded by community pressures from voting in local elections were protected by federal law in exercising their right to vote in NLRB elections. In company towns, employees who had never before enjoyed any voice in shaping their working lives cast ballots.

Some early Wagner Act elections involved industrial giants that had engaged in intermittent warfare with unions for decades. On May 21, 1941, following a bitter strike at the mammoth River Rouge plant, an NLRB election was held in which seventy-two thousand Ford Motor Company employees selected the United Automobile Workers of the CIO as their bargaining agent. This election followed a 5-year period during which the NLRB found that Ford had illegally discharged 2,566 workers and incurred a back-pay liability of $2 million. After this election, Ford and the UAW entered into a collective bargaining agreement that was distinctly the best that union had ever executed.

Prior to 1939, the Board occasionally accepted authorization cards and petitions signed by employees as proof that a union had been selected as a majority bargaining agent by employees. In that year, however, the Board became convinced that elections were more reliable than other means of determining employee wishes and adopted a policy of refusing to certify unions, unless they prevailed in secret-ballot elections.

The Labor Act's principle of majority rule is basic and simple, but its administration has always been complex and controversial. The discussion that follows is not intended as a definitive or comprehensive statement about NLRB election issues; it is, instead, a brief summary of only a few long-term issues. A large and growing body of technical literature discusses each of these in far greater detail.

APPROPRIATE BARGAINING UNITS

The Board does not conduct elections among random groups of employees—its critics might find this generalization unacceptable—but only among employees who form a unit that is "appropriate for the purposes of collective bargaining." This concept was first expressed in the Wagner Act and was retained, with several specific guidelines, by the Taft-Hartley Act. The appropriate bargaining-unit principle is set forth in Section 9(b) of the Act, and it is widely regarded as one of the broadest grants of discretion that Congress has entrusted to any administrative agency.

Congress directed the NLRB to make unit determinations on a case-by-case basis, subject only to the overriding mandate that units must "assure to employees the fullest freedom in exercising the rights guaranteed by this Act." Since 1935, the NLRB has struggled to define rational standards by which to exercise this discretion. Although most believe that the Board's successes exceed its failures, this difficult task has been accompanied by unceasing controversy.

Four basic categories of units are normally approved by the Board, with endless variations from industry to industry and employer to employer:

1. *Employer unit.* An employer unit normally includes *all* employees of a single enterprise, excluding supervisors, guards, and professional employees. Some employer units embrace all employees of nationwide corporations with tens of thousands of employees. But most such units involve smaller, local employers.

2. *Craft unit.* A craft unit is one that consists solely of skilled craftsmen, excluding all others. While, at first blush, it might seem perfectly simple to define such a unit, the Board's experience with craft units has shown the task to be far from easy. What is a craft? How much and what kind of training is required to justify the designation of craftsman? Should apprentices be included in the same unit with journeymen? Are sophisticated technicians, who have mastered the technologies of the computer age, craftsmen, or are they something else? Should a distinction be drawn between craft and craft-like skills? And should an election be conducted in a craft unit at the request of *any* labor organization or only an organization of craftsmen? Difficult though these questions have been for the Board, it has been even more difficult to decide when craftsmen should be granted the right to a separate election among themselves and when they should be grouped in a broader bargaining unit with noncraftsmen.

3. *Plant unit.* A plant unit, as distinguished from a multi-

plant unit, is simply the employees of one plant. Many employers have only one plant; others operate a number of plants that may engage in diverse functions. When is it appropriate to hold an election in only a single plant of a multiplant firm? When should all, or some, of the plants of such a firm be grouped together?

4. *Other units.* The fourth unit choice that Congress identified is a "subdivision thereof"—meaning a subdivision of an employer, craft, or plant unit. This alternative is virtually open-ended. It authorizes the Board, in proper cases, to direct elections among employees who work in department units, share a common supervisor, work in a defined geographic region, or even have in common the fact that they are the only remaining unrepresented employees in a plant.

Finally, *multi-employer* units may be established by the parties themselves, although the Board will not create them initially.

From its earliest experiences with unit problems, the Board has recognized the importance of experimentation and flexibility. Each industry has unique employment and administrative characteristics that must be weighed in establishing units, and, within a single industry, individual firms differ in significant ways, requiring special consideration in shaping units. Moreover, industrial change and collective bargaining practices have, from time to time, dictated re-evaluation of older unit policies in the light of contemporary realities.

The Board has been required to balance the statutory requirement that it make unit decisions on a case-by-case basis with the underlying policy mandate that unit decisions be rational and predictable. Striking this balance has always been a delicate problem, for unions and employers alike have strong and highly partisan views on unit issues. How, then, does the Board go about making a unit determination?

In 1937, the Board's second annual report explained:

Self-organization among employees is generally grounded in a community of interest in their occupations and more particularly in their qualifications, experience, duties, wages, hours and other working conditions. This community of interest may lead to organization along craft lines, along industrial lines, or in any of a number of other forms representing adaptations to special circumstances. The complexity of modern industry, transportation, and communication, and the numerous and diverse forms which self-organization among employees can take and has taken, preclude the application of rigid rules to the determination of the unit appropriate for the purposes of collective bargaining.

The "community of interest" concept has been the Board's guiding principle throughout the years.

The Practical Import of Units

The NLRB's unit decisions are often technical, if not simply boring to the layman. One cannot imagine many readers who, on a cold winter's night, would curl up before the fireplace with a volume of the NLRB's decisions to explore the mystery of whether truck drivers will be included in the same unit with production workers, whether editorial employees of a newspaper will be included in the same unit with commercial employees, or whether employees who repair ships will be included in the same unit with employees who repair shipping docks. These are familiar, old-fashioned unit problems for the NLRB.

To the parties involved, however, these issues are singularly important. They understand well the twofold importance of unit issues: First, the composition of the unit may strongly affect whether or not the union will win the election, because unions and employers have reliable sources of information about the inclinations of employees long before a secret-ballot election is held. Second, the composition of the unit may determine whether effective collective bargaining can ensue.

Obviously, unions always request a unit composed of employees who, they believe, are likely to vote in favor of union representation, while employers normally prefer units composed of employees who are likely to vote against union representation. This is, to be sure, an oversimplification of an immensely complex subject, but it helps to explain the importance that the parties attach to bargaining-unit issues. It also helps to explain the bitterness and complaints of those whose unit positions are rejected by the Board.

An example will illustrate this point. In the town of Centerville, there is a chain of five drug stores owned by the XYZ Corporation. The employees in one of the five stores decide that they want union representation, but the employees in the other four stores do not. The employees of the first store then seek a union to represent them. The union will ask them to sign authorization cards. With these, which are necessary to make the 30 per cent showing of interest, the union files an election petition requesting that the Board conduct an election in the single store. The union believes that it can easily win an election in a single-store unit. The employer may oppose this proposed unit, however, arguing that all five stores should be grouped together for an election.

Both the union and the employer can make intelligent arguments based on the community of interest doctrine to support their respective positions. The union maintains that employees in the single store share common supervision, work at a common site, are rarely interchanged with employees in the other four stores, and so forth. The employer argues that the five stores are operated as a single economic unit, that they have a common general manager, that personnel matters are handled from a central office, and that working conditions at all stores are identical.

If the Board directs an election in the single-store unit, the union's chances of winning the election are good. If, however, the Board rules against the union's requested unit and agrees with the employer that only a 5-store unit is appropriate, the union's election petition will be dismissed, and there will be no election at all.

The Board has decided hundreds of such cases in the retail industry, sometimes in favor of single-store and sometimes multistore units, depending on the particular facts.

Craft vs. Industrial Units

One of the ironies of the Board's history is that the internecine conflict between the AFL and the CIO coincided with the passage of the Wagner Act and the birth of the NLRB. Inevitably, the Board found itself in the center of a triangular struggle between craft unions, industrial unions, and employers.

The historian Broadus Mitchell has accurately summarized the Board's delicate position between the warring factions of the labor movement during the Wagner Act era:

> The fierce contest often lodged in the responsibility of the National Labor Relations Board to determine, in a given situation, what was the proper bargaining unit, and to rule on which union was to represent the workers. Especially in the beginning, claims of the C.I.O. embraced all of the employees in a plant without regard to particular processes, while the Federation was jealous of distinctions of craft. This antithesis made the work of the Board, operating under a discretionary mandate, difficult in the best case, but the heat and deceptions engendered in disputes rendered it doubly so. The result was that both sides accused the Board of flagrant favoritism, and interested employers and their national associations were quick to improve the opportunity to level their own charges. Proposals were made for amendment of the Wagner Act which would have bent it to endorse one form of unionism or the other, or which would have excluded large classes of workers from protection. . . . Other changes were urged under the guise of reform when the purpose was to destroy the law.

As time went by, the Board experimented with a variety of approaches to the question of craft vs. industrial units, while recognizing, as the Board said in a 1937 press release, that it "could not satisfy both litigants while they are engaged in what is to them a bitter and decisive struggle."

Perhaps the most important and enduring of the Board's early efforts to balance the competing interests of craft and industrial workers was reflected in the 1937 "*Globe* election" doctrine. This concept takes its name from a case in which two craft unions sought separate craft elections, while an industrial union sought an over-all industrial unit. The Board carefully weighed the factors that tended to favor separate craft units and those that supported an over-all industrial unit and concluded that they were so "evenly balanced" that either unit would be appropriate. Therefore, the Board directed *two* separate elections: Employees in the craft units were given the opportunity to vote for the craft union, for the industrial union, or for neither. If a majority of them favored the craft union, that union would be certified for the craft unit, on the theory that the craftsmen themselves favored the smaller unit. If, however, they voted against representation by the craft union, it would be assumed that they favored a larger unit or none. Their votes in this circumstance would then be pooled and counted with the votes in the larger unit of non-craftsmen to determine whether employees in the industrial unit wished to be represented by the union that sought to represent them on this basis.

Although the *Globe* doctrine was an inventive solution to a stubborn problem, it was far from perfect, for members of the Board frequently disagreed on how to determine when the factors were "evenly balanced."

Still more difficult for the Board has been the decades-old problem known as "craft severance." This issue arises when employees have been organized on an industrial basis and, thereafter, a small group of craft workers seeks to break away for purposes of separate representation by a craft union. Not only has this problem produced sharp conflict within the labor movement, it has frequently led to sharp disagreements within the Board. The question is simple: Under what circumstances should the NLRB direct an election to permit craftsmen to be severed from an industrial unit? The Board has answered this question differently in different decades:

In 1939, the Board issued its famous *American Can Company* decision, reasoning that it was not in the interest of stable labor relations to permit craft severance after a history of harmonious bargaining had been established on an industrial basis. This doctrine enraged the AFL. During the early 1940's, the Board established an exception to the *American Can* doctrine in cases where craftsmen had maintained their "craft identity" during the period of bargaining conducted on an industrial basis. The AFL still complained.

Congress considered this problem in 1947, and in the Taft-Hartley Act, Congress, through an amendment to Section 9(b) (2), provided that "the Board shall . . . not decide that any craft unit is inappropriate . . . on the ground that a different unit has been established by a prior Board determination, unless a majority of the employees in the proposed craft unit vote against separate representation." The AFL rejoiced at this legislation, somewhat prematurely.

In 1948, the Board was requested to permit severance of bricklayers in the steel industry. The Board dismissed the craft severance petition, on the grounds that the Taft-Hartley Amendments precluded reliance on prior Board determinations as the only basis for denying craft severance; it did not prevent the Board from considering its own prior determinations as *one* basis for a decision. The steel industry, the Board concluded, was marked by a high degree of "functional integration." Moreover, industrial bargaining had been successful in this industry, whereas fragmenting the broader unit might lead to instability. This doctrine, known as the "*National Tube*" doctrine, effectively denied craft severance in the steel industry. In subsequent cases, the Board applied this concept to several other industries—wet milling, lumber, and aluminum—because they, too, were "functionally integrated."

In 1954, however, the Board looked at this issue again. In the prominent *American Potash & Chemical Corporation* case, the Board established new, liberalized criteria for granting craft severance elections. Now, said the NLRB, it would direct such an election in cases where the petitioning union could show that the workers it sought to represent were regarded as true craftsmen and that the union was a traditional representative of such employees. Prior bargaining history and integration of operations, the Board implied, would no longer be seriously considered in such cases, although the Board declined to change its *National Tube* doctrine in the four industries to which it had been extended.

In 1966, prompted in some measure by a court rejection of the automatic severance rule, the NLRB considered this issue once more, and, in the *Mallinckrodt Chemical Works* case, it fashioned another approach to craft severance, largely rejecting the 1954 *American Potash* doctrine as both rigid and arbitrary. Instead, the Board announced a more eclectic and flexible approach, requiring a case-by-case determination of the suitability of severance, based on six broad criteria:

1. Whether the proposed unit consists of distinct and homogeneous, skilled craftsmen.
2. Whether the history of bargaining has been stable and successful and whether severance might be unduly disruptive.
3. Whether the craftsmen had maintained their separate identity.
4. The history and patterns of bargaining in the industry.
5. The degree of integration in the industry.
6. The qualifications of the union seeking a severed unit.

This doctrine, the Board announced, would be applied in the

future to all industries, including those that had previously been covered by the *National Tube* doctrine.

Mallinckrodt has found favor with industrial unions, as well as with many employers who believe that stability is more likely to be achieved in broad-based, rather than splintered, bargaining units. Craft unions were, and continue to be, displeased.

Is there any long-term solution to this conflict over craft units? Has the Board acted wisely in its formulation and application of *Mallinckrodt*? The answers turn largely on one's emphases. For example, if one places the heaviest possible emphasis on the Act's policy to promote industrial stability and successful collective bargaining, *Mallinckrodt* is undoubtedly a sound decision. On the other hand, if one primarily values the Act's encouragement of employee freedom of choice, one can just as rationally conclude that *Mallinckrodt* is unsound, because it deprives craftsmen of free choice to be separated from broader representation.

Congress could have resolved this issue once and for all by clear legislation. It chose not to, leaving the Board with the problem of reconciling the policy of industrial stability with the competing policy of employee free choice.

While the Board's changes in position are perhaps most dramatically illustrated by the craft severance cases, there have been periodic revisions in the Board's views about many other kinds of unit issues. Professional observers of the Board's unit decisions are quick to find fault with changes of policy, but the inherent subjectivity of these decisions makes change all but inevitable. Those who approach this matter with historical perspective find abundant evidence that periodic changes are not of profound magnitude. It is more important that the Board's unit determinations have provided and continue to provide the opportunity for millions of workers over a period of decades to cast a secret, uncoerced ballot in representation elections and to establish representation rights and recognition duties that lead to successful collective bargaining.

Protecting the Integrity of the Election Process

NLRB elections are patterned on the familiar election of public officials: They include such traditional election safeguards as carefully prepared eligibility lists, the opportunity for each participant to have an observer throughout the voting and counting processes, full protection of ballot secrecy, and the like.

In one significant respect, however, NLRB elections are quite different. Candidates for public office are legally free to conduct their campaigns virtually as they see fit. Subject only to the laws of libel, candidates for office may make false statements about themselves and their opponents, may make false and extravagant promises and predictions, and may even engage in trickery against their opponents. It is assumed that in elections for public office the voters will be able to sort out the real from the false and also that the competitive process will deter certain kinds of reprehensible behavior. But in Labor Board elections, if one party engages in conduct that impairs employee free choice, the Board may set the election aside and direct a new one.

The NLRB has a statutory duty to assure that its elections are conducted free from improper interference of the type that might be legally acceptable in public elections, because employers and, sometimes, unions *do* have direct economic power over the life of employee voters. Both the Board and courts have long recognized, for example, that statements by employers to employees carry special weight and meaning; employees know that an employer has the economic power to discharge and otherwise harm them economically. Thus, words spoken by an employer have a cutting edge much sharper than words spoken by candidates for public office. As the Supreme Court said in a 1940 decision, "Silent suggestions as to the employer's choice between unions may have telling effect among men who know the consequences of incurring that employer's strong displeasure." And, during the Wagner Act's early years, the Board required employers to maintain a position of strict neutrality during election campaigns.

In 1941, however, the Supreme Court considered the impact of the Constitution's protection of free speech rights on the Labor Act. In a leading decision, the Court ruled that an employer's expressions on the subject of unionism are protected free speech, unless they are coercive. With this standard as its guide, the Board liberalized its views about permissible employer speech during election campaigns.

Among the Taft-Hartley Amendments was one designed to insure that the Board would not treat noncoercive statements as evidence of an unfair labor practice. This provision, Section 8(c), essentially incorporated the Supreme Court's 1941 Constitutional decision into the statute.

Against this background, the Board has faced a very sensitive problem in decision-making: On the one hand, the Board may not inhibit legitimate, noncoercive expressions of opinion by employers or unions; on the other hand, the Board is obliged to protect its election processes from statements and actions that improperly interfere with employee free choice. Where should the line be drawn?

The Board has held that the Constitutional stricture of Section 8(c) applies—by its own terms—only to unfair labor practice cases, not to election interference cases that do not include an unfair labor practice charge. Of course, if speech or conduct does constitute an unfair labor practice under Section 8, it is coercive by definition and may constitute grounds for setting aside an election.

In 1948, the Board laid down a very broad test by which to judge conduct alleged to have interfered with the conduct of an election: *"In election proceedings, it is the Board's function to provide a laboratory in which an experiment may be conducted, under conditions as nearly ideal as possible, to determine the uninhibited desires of the employees. . . ."* This is one of the classic sentences in all of labor-relations law. In hundreds of cases each year, the Board judges an infinite variety of statements and conduct by this standard.

During the decade of the Eisenhower Board, election statements were given maximum latitude, but, in the years thereafter, the Board gave more substance to the laboratory test and strove to examine campaign statements more critically in the interest of protecting employee free choice.

A number of campaign rules are objective and easily followed by the parties. For example, one rule flatly prohibits so-called captive audience meetings of employees within twenty-four hours of an election; this rule guarantees that employees will have at least one full day to consider their election choice without being required to listen to campaign arguments. Another protective rule prohibits campaign activity too close to polling places. Still another requires an employer to provide parties with the names and addresses of voters within seven days after an election has been directed, so that all parties may have a more equal opportunity to communicate with employee voters.

Other problems related to the conduct of elections, such as use of the employer's premises for electioneering, are far more difficult. When and under what circumstances may an employer preclude his own employees or outside union organizers from distributing union literature and discussing campaign issues on the employer's privately owned property? The Board has long held that an employer may not interfere with the right of employees to communicate about unions at the workplace on their own time but that an employer is entitled to prohibit such communication between employees during working hours: "Working time is for work," the Board has said. These rulings strike a balance between the employer's right to control his private property in a reasonable way and the protection of the statutory right of employees to engage in union activities in the most convenient and natural location, the workplace.

Professional union organizers, on the other hand, have less

access to the employer's premises for campaign purposes than employees. This issue is so important and complex that it has reached the Supreme Court's attention on several occasions. In one leading decision, *NLRB* v. *Babcock & Wilcox,* the Court ruled that an employer may exclude nonemployee organizers from his privately owned parking lot, if the employer applies this policy in a nondiscriminatory fashion *and* if the circumstances afford alternative means of communicating with employees through reasonable efforts. This strikes a balance between property rights of the employer and Section 7 rights of employees in a manner calculated to protect and respect both. For the Board, it has not been easy to apply this decision in particular cases. Opinions differ over the *adequacy* of alternative means of communication, and no simple formula can be devised to resolve such cases. Each must be decided in the light of its unique factual configuration.

There are a number of special applications of the *Babcock & Wilcox* rule that illustrate the many aspects of the Board's responsibility in protecting employee free choice. If the employer operates a remote logging camp that is located on private property, and if employees live in the camp for many months at a time, the employer may not exercise his rights as a property owner to insulate employees from union contacts. Similarly, the Board has held that owners of ocean vessels and operators of vacation resorts may not invoke private property rights as a barrier between employees living and working on the employer's premises and union organizers.

Perhaps the most difficult responsibility of the Board in protecting the integrity of elections concerns its scrutiny of the parties' campaign speeches and written materials. While wishing to avoid censorship and undue restrictions on the parties' opportunity to engage in vigorous campaigning, the Board, nonetheless, has a public obligation to assure that employee voters are not subject to grossly unfair campaign tactics. And this often requires drawing fine lines.

In its well-known *Hollywood Ceramics* case of 1962, the

Board set forth guidelines for dealing with campaign trickery and misrepresentations. For example, on the evening before a scheduled election, the union distributes a handbill that states that its collective agreement with the employer's major competitor provides for an average hourly wage of $4.50 per hour, $.75 higher than the wages of the employees who are to vote the next day. Of course, the handbill implies that, by voting for the union, employees can expect the union to negotiate a contract providing them with an increase of $.75 an hour. Employees who have been undecided about how to cast their ballot might be persuaded by this handbill to vote for the union at the last minute. If, however, the union's handbill is a gross and calculated misrepresentation and, in fact, the union's contract with the employer's competitor provides for an average hourly wage of only $4 per hour, employees have been misled. The lateness of the distribution of the handbill precludes the employer's responding to the misrepresentation, and the employee voters would not have the independent knowledge to see through the union's misrepresentation. If the union wins the election under these circumstances, should it be certified as the exclusive bargaining agent of employees? In this example, undoubtedly, the Board's decision in *Hollywood Ceramics* would require that the election be set aside. The Board declared in that case:

> [An] election should be set aside only where there has been a misrepresentation or other similar campaign trickery, which involves a substantial departure from the truth, at a time which prevents the other party or parties from making an effective reply, so that the misrepresentation, whether deliberate or not, may reasonably be expected to have a significant impact on the election.

A still more vexatious problem concerns the thin line between threats and predictions. If an employer tells his employees that he will close his business if they select a union to represent them, that is unquestionably a threat; it would violate Section 8(a) (1) and would be grounds for setting aside an election. If, however, the employer merely expresses his opinion that the probable impact of their voting for a union will be to raise his labor costs and force up the price of his products, thereby making him uncompetitive, and, in turn, causing him to go out of business, the situation is less clear. Is there a meaningful difference between the undisguised threat to go out of business in retaliation against voting for a union and the prediction that voting for a union might require the employer to go out of business? The effect of these statements might, in fact, be very similar on employees fearful that voting for a union may jeopardize their jobs.

The First Amendment of the Constitution and Section 8(c) of the Labor Act protect noncoercive expressions of opinion, and, therefore, the Board approaches employer predictions with care. The First Amendment protects speech, regardless of the identity of the speaker. And the Board, notwithstanding some of its critics, has evidenced a long-term commitment to the proposition that employees are entitled to hear full discussion of the issues raised during an organizing campaign.

Nevertheless, the First Amendment and Section 8(c) are not a shield to be wrapped around statements that, no matter how artfully worded in the form of predictions, effectively communicate coercive threats. The Board, thus, looks to the circumstances surrounding economic predictions to ascertain whether that context taints the predictions with a quality of coercion. This is often known as the "totality of conduct" doctrine, and, until 1969, it met with an uneven reception in the courts. In that year, however, a major prediction case reached the Supreme Court. The Board had found that an employer's prediction of economic harm was coercive, because it had been made in conjunction with many other statements that, in their totality, conveyed a very clear message to employees: If you vote for the union, this plant will probably close down. To the Board, this threat violated employee rights, even though the precise form of words—standing alone—expressed only a prediction.

The Supreme Court agreed with the Board. Speaking for the Court, Chief Justice Earl Warren—in his last labor-relations opinion before retirement—said:

> Any assessment of the precise scope of an employer expression, of course, must be made in the context of its labor relations setting. . . . Thus, an employer is free to communicate to his employees any of his general views about unionism or any of his specific views about a particular union, so long as the communications do not contain a "threat of reprisal or force or promise of benefit." He may even make a prediction as to the precise effects he believes unionization will have on his company. In such a case, however, the prediction must be carefully phrased on the basis of objective fact to convey an employer's belief as to demonstrably probable consequences beyond his control or to convey a management decision already arrived at. . . . If there is any implication that an employer may or may not take action solely on his own initiative for reasons unrelated to economic necessities and known only to him, the statement is no longer a reasonable prediction based on available facts but a threat of retaliation based on misrepresentation and coercion, and as such without the protection of the First Amendment. . . . [An] employer is free only to tell "what he reasonably believes will be the likely economic consequences of unionization that are outside his control," and not "threats of economic reprisal to be taken solely on his own volition."

VIII

Unfair Labor Practices
in Perspective

The Wagner Act established the bedrock national labor policy that employees are entitled to engage in self-organization, collective bargaining, and concerted activities. To protect these rights, Congress prohibited five kinds of employer conduct, the original five unfair labor practices. The Taft-Hartley Act broadened the national labor policy by guaranteeing also the right of employees "to refrain" from self-organization, collective bargaining, and concerted activities, and it added six union unfair labor practices. Landrum-Griffin added a seventh union unfair labor practice and a prohibition against both employers and unions who enter into "hot cargo" agreements.

Because this volume has been written for the general reader, rather than the legal specialist, many significant but technical aspects of the law of unfair labor practices will not be discussed in this chapter. There are, however, excellent treatises and casebooks that deal extensively with the entire field of unfair labor practices. The bibliography at the end of this volume may be a useful guide to those who wish to explore the field in greater depth.

THIRTEEN UNFAIR LABOR
PRACTICES, SUMMARIZED

Employers shall not

8(a)	(1)	Interfere with, coerce, or restrain employees.
8(a)	(2)	Assist or dominate labor organizations.
8(a)	(3)	Discriminate against employees to discourage or encourage union membership, except that a lawful union security clause may be signed.
8(a)	(4)	Discriminate against employees because they have given testimony or filed charges with the Board.
8(a)	(5)	Refuse to bargain in good faith with a majority union.

Unions shall not

8(b)	(1)	Coerce or restrain employees or interfere with management's choice of a bargaining agent.
8(b)	(2)	Cause an employer to discriminate against employees illegally.
8(b)	(3)	Refuse to bargain in good faith with an employer.
8(b)	(4)	Engage in secondary boycotts or jurisdictional strikes.
8(b)	(5)	Charge excessive or discriminatory initiation fees.
8(b)	(6)	Engage in featherbedding.
8(b)	(7)	Engage in organization or recognition picketing.

Neither employers nor unions shall

8(e)		Enter "hot cargo" agreements.

Each of these unfair labor practices was enacted by Congress after hearings, study, and debate. Each reflects a "vice" in labor-management relations that Congress was determined, in the public interest, to stop. To put it somewhat differently, Congress wanted to prevent employers from discharging employees because they engage in union activity, to prevent unions from engaging in secondary boycotts, and so forth. The NLRB was created to police those practices of the labor-relations community that violate Congress's proscriptions.

But the United States is a large country, and the NLRB is a small agency. Was Congress realistic in placing such a formidable enforcement burden on the Board? In 1935, no one could answer that question with any confidence.

If America's tens of thousands of employers and labor organizations chose to disregard the law, the NLRB could not enforce it with a staff of one hundred thousand agents. Congress's labor policies are enforceable, because the vast majority of employers and unions obey the law voluntarily, just as the nation's tax laws are enforceable, because most citizens are fundamentally law-abiding. There are, after all, nations in which labor and tax laws are unenforceable, because their citizens neither respect nor fear the law.

Derek Bok and John Dunlop have observed:

> Perhaps the most significant characteristic of the American collective bargaining system is that it is highly decentralized. There are approximately 150,000 separate union-management agreements now in force in the United States. A majority of union members work under contracts negotiated by their union with a single employer or for a single plant. Only 40 percent of employees covered by collective agreements involve multi-employer negotiations, and the great bulk of these negotiations are confined to single metropolitan areas. . . .
>
> The prevalence of plant and company negotiations in the United States is a natural outgrowth of the patterns of organization among employees and unions, the great size of this country, and the highly competitive character of its economy.

An inevitable result of the decentralization of union organization and collective bargaining in the United States is that labor-relations attitudes and practices vary enormously from industry to industry and from firm to firm. In appraising the NLRB's administration of the unfair labor practice provisions of the law—almost four decades after the passage of the Wagner Act and almost three decades after the passage of Taft-Hartley—it is useful to bear in mind that most employers and unions understand the law and voluntarily obey its mandates. A much smaller group is badly informed and may violate the law through ignorance. Still a third group, doubtless the smallest minority, understands the law but, nonetheless, violates it consciously to gain some strategic advantage.

Although the unfair labor practice features of the Labor Act have been interpreted and clarified in many major respects, with the result that the parties can usually ascertain their legal obligations, labor relations is a highly dynamic and ever-changing field of activity: Technology develops constantly; corporations and unions continually alter their forms of organization; issues and procedures at the bargaining table change dramatically from decade to decade; and new social, economic, and legal forces of society at large create varying pressures on labor and management. For these reasons, the law itself is not static, and the Board is called upon to interpret and apply the unfair labor practice provisions of the Act to a seemingly infinite variety of new industrial-relations practices.

These background considerations help to explain the nature of the Board's work in the unfair labor practice area, particularly the persistence of routine violations, the great diversity of issues, and the constant emergence of new issues.

In the sections that follow, several major unfair labor practice provisions have been singled out for discussion to indicate the sweep of the Board's work. No effort has been made, however, to deal with even these provisions comprehensively. Rather, from the thousands of formal decisions of the NLRB and the courts, only a handful of particularly interesting and significant ones have been culled out for purposes of illustration.

Protection of Section 7 Rights Against Coercion, Restraint, Interference, and Discrimination

Sections 8(a) (1) and 8(b) (1) protect employees from coercion, restraint, or interference with the employees' Section 7 rights by employers and unions, respectively. Sections 8(a) (3) and 8(b) (2) protect employees from discrimination. During the Board's long history, in the course of deciding thousands of such cases, several major categories of employer and union conduct have emerged as extremely important.

Coercion: Employer Actions

Violence. By far the least common, but most pernicious, interference with employee rights involves the use of violence against employees and union organizers. Today, this is an exceedingly rare problem, but in the early days of the Wagner Act it was common for employer groups to engage in systematic campaigns of terrorism against union organizers and employee leaders. Of course, violent assaults on the person usually violate state and local laws as well. However, occasionally, local law enforcement officials are themselves participants in such assaults or are reluctant to incur the displeasure of local citizens who commit such assaults. Therefore, a federal prohibition against assaults on union adherents is significant.

As recently as 1968, the Special Subcommittee on Labor of the U.S. House of Representatives conducted a series of hearings on the Labor Act's remedies. In its final report, the subcommittee observed: "Some of the most shocking testimony before the Subcommittee concerned the brutality and violence sometimes used to deny employees their statutory right to self-organization." The subcommittee documented two particularly brutal cases in Mississippi and Georgia, and its report confirmed the Board's experience that infrequent instances of violence against employees and union organizers in recent years typically occur in rural Southern towns.

Espionage and Surveillance. Employees are entitled to engage in union activities without coming under the surveillance of their employers. Again, in the early years of the Wagner Act, surveillance and espionage carried out against employees were common; they have become less so in recent decades. It is unlawful for employers to plant a spy in union meetings, to observe who attends union meetings, to pay employees to supply information to the employer, or to give employees the impression that they are under surveillance.

Although this is no longer a widespread problem, the McClellan committee's hearings in 1957 revealed that a few major corporations continued to employ the services of so-called labor-relations consultants whose specialties included espionage activities during union organizing campaigns. In the typical surveillance case today, a supervisor sits across the street from a union meeting hall and systematically records the automobile license numbers of employees who drive up to attend a union meeting. Whether employees are aware of the supervisor's presence or not, such conduct is wholly illegal. A dramatic claim of employer use of electronic listening devices against textile union organizers was disclosed in the summer of 1973 by a $50 million damage suit against the textile firm J. P. Stevens & Company, a frequent respondent in NLRB cases.

Threats. Threatening employees with any kind of direct or indirect harm or loss of benefits is plainly prohibited by Section 8(a) (1). While such violations today tend to be less crude than in the 1930's, they persist with astonishing frequency. The classic threat to an employee is that he will be fired, if he engages in union activities. There are many variations: Threats that employees will be demoted, not promoted, suffer a wage reduction, be denied overtime opportunities, have their total hours of work reduced, cause the employer to relocate or close his plant, be locked out, be forced to go on strike, or lose fringe benefits are typical. Some NLRB cases have been based on threats involving virulent racism; for example, white workers have been threatened that they will be replaced by black workers.

Promises of Benefit. Promising or actually granting benefits to employees to discourage union activity is prohibited by the Labor Act. The reason for this was explained in a major Supreme Court decision in 1964:

> The danger inherent in well-timed increases is the suggestion of a fist inside the velvet glove. Employees are not likely to miss the inference that the source of benefits now conferred is also the source from which future benefits must flow and which may dry up if it is not obliged. . . .
>
> The beneficence of an employer is likely to be ephemeral if prompted by a threat of unionization which is subsequently removed. Insulating the right of collective organization from calculated good will of this sort deprives employees of little that has lasting value.

The Board views promises or grants of new benefits during an organizing campaign as a form of bribery to deprive employees of statutory rights. If an employer granted an employee an annual wage increase of $100, it would be as illegal as offering that employee the same amount of cash to refrain from union activity.

Of course, not all promises of benefit are prohibited during organizing campaigns, only those that, by their nature, are intended to interfere with Section 7 rights.

Interrogation. Congress provided secret-ballot election machinery for the purpose of permitting employees to decide, free from coercion, whether they wish to be represented for purposes of collective bargaining. Implicit in the secret-ballot election process is the assumption that employees should not be required to disclose to their employer how they feel about him or unions in general. From the earliest days of the Wagner Act, therefore, the Board has interpreted Section 8(a) (1) to prohibit systematic interrogation of employees about their views in this sensitive area. An employer may not ask employees how they intend to vote, whether they have engaged in union activities, which fellow workers are union leaders, what the union's plans are, or similar questions.

A more complex issue concerns the polling of employees by different methods and whether this practice interferes with Section 7 rights. Over the years, as different Boards have approached the subject with different philosophies and on the basis of varying court decisions, the Board's views on this subject have changed. In its well-known *Struksnes Construction Company* decision, the Board defined the standards that must be observed by management in conducting a poll of employees:

> Absent unusual circumstances, the polling of employees . . . will be violative of . . . the Act unless the following safeguards are observed: (1) the purpose of the poll is to determine the truth of a union's claim of majority, (2) this purpose is communicated to the employees, (3) assurances against reprisal are given, (4) the employees are polled by secret ballot, and (5) the employer has not engaged in unfair labor practices or otherwise created a coercive atmosphere.

Solicitation and Distribution Rules. Employees are entitled to discuss issues related to union representation and to receive information about it, for such communication is a vital feature of the right to engage in self-organization and concerted activities. Many limitations on methods of employee communication are illegal, typically rules that broadly prohibit discussing union issues during employee free periods, distributing literature to employees, wearing union badges and insignia, attending union meetings, and other such activities.

It is perfectly clear, however, that the right of employees to communicate about unions and to engage in union activities must not deprive management of its equally legitimate right to require employees to work during working hours and to prevent interference with the reasonable conduct of business.

Sometimes, these rights of employees and management clash, and the Board's obligation is to reconcile them. For example, the Board has held that employees normally are entitled to wear union insignia during working hours. The employer may require that such insignia be removed, however, if they might be caught in machinery and thereby cause a safety hazard. Employees have the right to distribute and receive union literature but not to litter the employer's premises. Employees have the right to talk about unionism on their own time but not when they are required to devote all of their energies to the employer's work.

The question of access to the employer's premises was discussed in Chapter VII in relationship to conduct that interferes with fair NLRB elections. That discussion is applicable here, too. Of particular importance is the Supreme Court's 1956 decision in *Babcock & Wilcox,* which held that an employer violates Section 8(a) (1) by excluding a non-employee organizer from a privately owned parking lot *only* if the union has no other adequate, alternative means of communication. In a 1972 decision, the Supreme Court had occasion to examine the *Babcock & Wilcox* principle of accommodation once again in a somewhat different context. The high Court affirmed that principle, but did so in language that hints that the "Nixon Court" of 1972 is less willing to require private property rights to be harmonized with Section 7 rights than was the "Warren Court" of 1956.

Coercion: Union Actions

Section 8(b) (1) (A) is roughly the counterpart of Section 8(a) (1), for it prohibits union restraint or coercion of employees in exercising their Section 7 rights. A variety of union actions fall within the ambit of Section 8(b) (1) (A); the most common examples involve mass picketing, picket-line violence, and threats of violence. Acts of violence by unions are relatively rare today, but they persist, particularly in tense strike situations.

Of course, state and local laws also protect employees from violence and threats of violence, but the federal law offers an additional remedy that, in some instances, is more effective.

Fines. A type of union coercion that has been the subject of considerable litigation in recent years concerns the imposition of fines on union members for violating union rules and policies. The Supreme Court in two recent cases has held that union fines are legitimate and may be enforced by unions in the courts against full members, if four conditions have been met:

1. The fine seeks to enforce a properly adopted union rule.
2. The rule in question is based on a valid union interest.
3. Imposition of the fine impairs no congressional policy.
4. The fine is imposed on members who are free to leave the union and thereby escape the rule.

Fines may not be enforced against union members under *any* circumstances by affecting their employment rights, only by expulsion from the union or by judicial enforcement.

The Supreme Court has also ruled that fines imposed on employees for seeking access to the Board itself are illegal, for Congress intended to guarantee the right of employees to have unencumbered access to the procedures of the NLRB.

In 1972, the Supreme Court ruled on another aspect of the union fine problem under Section 8(b) (1). This case, *NLRB* v. *Granite State Joint Board, Textile Workers,* involved a group of union members who voted in favor of a strike, participated in the strike, but later decided to resign from the union and return to work, while the strike was still in progress. They were fined $2,000 each by their union, which sought to collect the fine by filing a lawsuit. The NLRB ruled that their resignations were valid under the union's constitution. Having severed their membership in the union, they were, therefore, free to return to work, and the imposition of a fine interfered with their statutory right "to refrain" from union activities. The Supreme Court agreed with the Board and upheld the unfair labor practice finding against the union.

In 1973, the Supreme Court ruled on the question of whether fines that otherwise have been properly imposed are illegal because they are excessive in amount. The Board has consistently ruled that it has no authority to review the reasonableness of union fines. If unions seek to enforce fines, the courts are authorized to deny enforcement to excessive fines, as, in fact, they frequently have. The court of appeals for the District of Columbia disagreed, however, with the Board's view on this subject. It ruled that the Board should establish national standards for determining the reasonableness of fines. The Supreme Court reversed that decision and agreed with the Board.

Close questions arise if the fined union member is also a supervisor, a common situation in some building and printing trades. The Board, with court support, has decided that such penalties violate Section 8(b) (1) (B), as coercion of an employer in the selection of his representatives. In cases where these fines are levied because the supervisor crosses the union picket line and performs struck work, however, the courts of appeals are divided.

The union fine cases illustrate the Board's role in protecting the rights of the individual union member from unwarranted interference by the group.

Discrimination

Section 8(a) (3) prohibits discrimination by management against employees to discourage or encourage membership in a union, except that employees may be required to join a labor union pursuant to the terms of a lawful union shop contract.* And, by parity, Section 8(b) (2) prohibits discrim-

* Under Section 8(a) (3) a union shop agreement is lawful if it requires employees to join a union no sooner than thirty days after their employment or after execution of the contract, whichever is later. There are other, technical requirements as well.

ination by labor organizations that would cause employers to violate Section 8(a) (3). In the simplest terms, these unfair labor practice provisions guarantee employees complete freedom from discrimination by employers or unions *related to* activities that either favor or disfavor unionism. These provisions have several highly complex legal dimensions, but the categories identified below are the most familiar and important.

Discharge. Before the Wagner Act, it was extraordinarily common for employers to fire workers who engaged in union activity; employees had no legal recourse whatever, except to strike. Unfortunately, after several decades, instances of discriminatory discharges are still common. In nearly two-thirds of the cases filed against employers in 1972, there were charges of such violations. Rarely does an employer admit that he has fired an employee for this reason; instead, such discharges are sometimes justified on other grounds—typically, poor productivity, misconduct, absenteeism, and the unavailability of work. Under the Act, an employer may terminate an employee's services for any reason *except* union activity. When an employee claims that his discharge was for an illegal reason, but his employer claims that the reason was legitimate, the Board scrutinizes all the circumstances surrounding the discharge to determine whether *one* reason for the discharge was discriminatory. Often uncovering an employer's motivation is a sensitive and difficult problem. For example, an employee who is an active union adherent may also have a poor work record and be discharged. If the employer's true reason for discharging the worker was his work record, the discharge is legal; if this reason was accompanied by the employer's desire to be rid of a union activist, the discharge is illegal.

Each case must be decided on its own facts, and rarely are two cases of this type identical. Over many years, and after deciding thousands of such cases, the Board has developed a series of evidentiary guidelines that indicate the possible presence of an illegal motive. Prominent among these are:

1. The discharge occurred shortly after the employer learned of an employee's union activity.
2. The employer had never discharged other employees for the same, asserted reason in the past.
3. The discharge occurred in the context of the employer's expressed hostility to unions or in the context of coercive threats.
4. The employer gave inconsistent explanations for the discharge.
5. The employer gave no reason whatever for the discharge.
6. The discharged employee had been illegally threatened or coerced in the past.
7. The stated reason for the discharge was obviously petty and inconsequential.
8. The employee had an excellent past record and had not previously been criticized.
9. The employee was singled out for discharge, while other employees were given lesser forms of discipline for the same actions.
10. The discharged employees were the only union activists in the firm.

A number of cases raise the question of whether employees were discharged for engaging in various kinds of concerted activities. Because Section 7 protects this right, such discharges are prohibited. One of the most interesting and important of the cases in this category, *NLRB* v. *Washington Aluminum Company,* was decided by the Supreme Court in 1962. Seven employees were discharged when they jointly left their jobs, complaining that the plant in which they worked was too cold. The workers had no union, but they acted in concert. The employer argued that it was entitled to fire these employees, because they left the plant without giving him an opportunity to discuss their complaint. Moreover, they violated a plant rule against leaving their jobs without permission.

The Board held that this walkout was a protected activity for which employees could not be discharged. A federal appellate court disagreed, and the NLRB appealed to the Supreme Court, which agreed with the Board. Justice Hugo Black, who wrote the Court's opinion, commented:

> Indeed, concerted activities by employees for the purpose of trying to protect themselves from working conditions as uncomfortable as the testimony and Board findings showed them to be in this case are unquestionably activities to correct conditions which modern labor-management legislation treats as too bad to have to be tolerated in a humane and civilized society like ours.

On the other hand, both the Board and the courts have held that the right to engage in concerted activities does not encompass the right to engage in such illegal actions as a mutiny at sea, a sit-down strike, a strike in violation of a contract's "no-strike" provision, or violence.

As a general rule, employees may not be discharged for engaging in a peaceful strike that does not violate an existing collective bargaining agreement. But, for many years, the Act has been interpreted to permit an employer to operate his business during an economic strike, and, as a concomitant, an employer is entitled to hire *permanent* replacements for economic strikers. Frequently, the Board is called to determine whether strike replacements are temporary or permanent. If the replacements are found to be temporary, the strikers are entitled to be reinstated to their former jobs when they make an unconditional request for reinstatement. Even if permanently replaced, economic strikers, under Board and court decisions of the late 1960's, do not lose their status as employees. On conclusion of their strike and at their request, they are thereafter entitled to preferential consideration for reinstatement as job vacancies open up. A different rule applies to unfair labor practice strikers, those who strike to protest an employer's unfair labor practices. They may not be permanently replaced and are always entitled to reinstatement on making an unconditional request.

Section 8(b) (2), which deals with union actions that cause an employer to discriminate against employees, is a less frequently used section of the law. It may be invoked when a union seeks to have an employer discharge or otherwise discriminate against an employee in a variety of situations, commonly when an employee has incurred a union's disfavor for some reason. It is the employee's shield against a union's imposition of a closed shop to bar his employment.

Lockouts. During the first thirty years of the Labor Act, the Board ruled that, ordinarily, an employer could not lock out his employees as an economic weapon to force the union to come to terms, except in several unique situations. However, in two major decisions in 1965, the Supreme Court—disagreeing with the Board—held that an employer does not violate Section 8(a)(3) when he locks out employees "solely in support of a legitimate bargaining position." Under these decisions, an employer may lock out employees to advance his position in bargaining, but he may not lock them out to discourage union activity, or before bargaining in good faith.

A number of questions have been raised by the Supreme Court's lockout decisions, and the Board has begun to resolve them on a case-by-case basis. The problem illustrates the dynamic character of the law; it is one of a number of major policy areas of the statute that has not been definitively explored, even after several decades.

Other Types of Discrimination. Virtually any harm that an employer or labor organization inflicts on employees to encourage or discourage union activity might violate Sections 8(a)(3) and 8 (b)(2). Listed below are examples of familiar types of discrimination in retaliation for union activity:

1. Closing a plant because employees vote for union representation.
2. Blacklisting union adherents.

3. Refusing to hire applicants for employment because of prior union activity.
4. Demoting or refusing to promote employees.
5. Reducing fringe benefits.
6. Withdrawing traditional overtime opportunities.
7. Depriving employees of customary wage increases.
8. Eliminating any customary rights or privileges in employment.
9. Laying off or otherwise depriving employees of opportunities to work.
10. Imposing more severe penalties for misconduct.
11. Supervising employee work with greater strictness and severity than has been customary.
12. Refusing to refer qualified workers to jobs from an exclusive union hiring hall because of nonmembership in the union.

THE DUTY TO BARGAIN IN GOOD FAITH

The pivotal policy of the Labor Act has been to promote and encourage collective bargaining. Congress sought to implement this policy in the Wagner Act through enactment of what is now Section 8(a)(5). As interpreted and refined, this provision requires employers to bargain in "good faith" with a majority bargaining agent of employees in an appropriate bargaining unit. In 1947, Congress enacted Section 8(b)(3), which extends the identical bargaining obligation to labor organizations.

The highly decentralized and largely local patterns of collective bargaining in America have produced widely differing practices and traditions, all of which have had to be accommodated under the broad policies of the statute. Some scholars have devoted years to studying the meaning of the bargaining obligation; obviously, the following discussion cannot deal with this subject comprehensively. Several basic concepts that have emerged from Board and court decisions indicate that the generalities of the law have been systematically translated into clear and legible guideposts.

"Good Faith"

The Wagner Act did not in so many words require that the parties bargain in good faith, but this concept was incorporated into the law through interpretation by the Board and courts. In 1947, Congress accepted these interpretations and, in Section 8(d), explicitly incorporated the good faith standard. But what does it mean, and how should it be applied to individual cases? Unquestionably, good faith is a subjective standard that looks to a party's *state of mind* at a precise point in time. The Board's historic task has been to fashion criteria that fairly reflect the presence or absence of this state of mind.

First, it is clear that Congress did not require one party to make concessions to the other. When Congress examined this problem in 1947, it declared flatly and explicitly in Section 8(d) that the duty to bargain in good faith "does not compel either party to agree to a proposal or require the making of a concession." Does this mean, however, that one party may simply sit back and say "no" to every proposal that the other makes? In one of its earliest Wagner Act cases, *Sands Manufacturing Company,* the Board indicated the philosophy that has consistently guided its decisions on this issue:

> Before the obligation to bargain is fulfilled, a forthright, candid effort must be made by the employer to reach a settlement of the dispute with his employees. Every avenue and possibility of negotiation must be exhausted before it should be admitted that an irreconcilable difference creating an impasse has been reached. Of course no general rule as to the process of collective bargaining can be made to apply to all cases. The process required varies with the circumstances in each case. But the effort at collective bargaining must be real and not merely apparent.

In many cases, the Board and courts have faced the problem of "surface bargaining," in which an employer would dutifully go through the *motions* of discussing every union proposal, never intending to reach agreement on any one of them. Does such conduct, which honors the formalities of the law but disregards its substance, constitute bad faith? The Board and courts have held that it does in countless instances where it could be proved that the employer's state of mind rejected the possibility of reaching an understanding with the bargaining agent of employees. But the problem of surface bargaining remains, and its case-by-case resolution has not been wholly satisfactory; perhaps it never will be.

The prestigious Labor Study Group of the Committee for Economic Development commented in 1961 that "it is unrealistic to expect that, by legislation, 'good faith' can be brought to the bargaining table." But what are the alternatives? Should Congress and the Board ignore the parties' subjective state of mind and permit them to avoid even the formal trappings of discussion, exchange of views, and exploration of bargainable issues? This solution seems to many far worse than the lingering problem of dealing with insincere, surface bargaining. Notwithstanding many indications of growing maturity in the collective bargaining process, we have not yet reached, and probably will never reach, the stage of ideal philosophical commitment by both parties to finding the fairest and most rational solution to problems.

Procedures of Good Faith Bargaining

Although it is difficult—often impossible—to ascertain a party's subjective state of mind at the bargaining table, Congress has legislated several minimum standards that the parties must observe. These were part of the Taft-Hartley Amendments and are contained in Section 8(d):

> For the purposes of this section, to bargain collectively is the performance of the mutual obligation . . . to meet at reasonable times and confer in good faith with respect to wages, hours,

and other terms and conditions of employment, . . . and the execution of a written contract incorporating any agreement reached if requested by either party.

At a minimum, therefore, Congress has directed the parties to meet at reasonable times and to execute in writing any agreement that the parties have reached. These objective standards for the performance of the good faith obligation have been expanded by the Board and courts in a number of cases:

1. The parties must meet at mutually convenient places.
2. The parties must be willing to devote a reasonable amount of time to the bargaining process.
3. The parties must be represented in bargaining by someone who has authority to speak for the principals and who is not merely a messenger.
4. The parties must reply to each other's proposals within a reasonable period of time.
5. The parties must not impose unfair conditions upon bargaining, such as the settlement of outstanding grievances or unfair labor practice charges.
6. The parties must not by-pass each other's designated representatives.
7. The parties must supply each other with such reasonable information as may be required to bargain rationally. For example, an employer cannot conceal from a union information about employees' wages or even wage surveys on which the employer's bargaining position rests. A leading decision of the Supreme Court in 1955 upheld the Board's view that an employer who claims financial inability to grant wage demands must submit substantiating information upon request.

To put this discussion in balance, it must be added that most employers and unions have developed their own mutually satisfactory and productive practices in bargaining. They rarely have occasion to bring their problems to the Board, but they are well acquainted with the standards that have been established by the NLRB and observe them faithfully and voluntarily. In this sense, the Labor Act and the Board's decisions provide clear guidance to countless thousands of negotiators each year in every industry and every region of the country; this is one of the little-noticed successes of the law and of the Board.

Subject Matter of Bargaining

Section 8(d) requires bargaining about wages, hours, and working conditions. What specific subjects are included in these broad categories of coverage? On a case-by-case basis, the Board and courts have provided the parties with a catalog of hundreds of individual items that must be discussed at the request of either party, and the list has grown as the parties themselves have chosen to explore new subjects in negotiations.

Of course many of the subjects about which the parties are required to bargain are economic in character. Prominent among these are direct wages, hours of work, overtime rates of pay, vacations, holidays, bonuses, incentive and piecework rates, health and life insurance, pensions, supplemental unemployment benefits, profit-sharing plans, and productivity. Other issues are primarily concerned with conditions governing the employment relationship: such as mandatory retirement ages, seniority rights, nondiscriminatory hiring practices, performance of work by supervisors, opportunities for promotion and transfer, layoff policies, work-sharing practices, training opportunities, and rest periods. A few subjects are of special importance to the union as an institution; examples include union security arrangements, the right to visit the workplace to assure that the contract is being honored, the right to process grievances through the arbitration stage, the right to be notified of personnel actions, and access to employee bulletin boards.

In its landmark 1958 *Wooster Division of Borg-Warner Corporation* decision, the Supreme Court sustained the Board's interpretation of the statute that all subjects should be divided into two categories: those that are embraced by the wages, hours, and working conditions coverage of Section 8(d), which are called "mandatory" subjects of bargaining; and those that are outside the coverage of Section 8(d), "permissive" or discretionary subjects of bargaining.

Each party, on request of the other, *must* bargain about mandatory subjects. But neither party may *insist* on bargaining about permissive subjects to the point of an impasse, although they may bargain about them voluntarily. Although Section 8(d) appears to require this dichotomy, many scholars believe it is highly artificial and that the law should permit the parties to insist on bargaining about all subjects of interest.

The *Borg-Warner* case itself dealt with an employer's insistence that a union agree to a prestrike vote on the employer's last offer and that the certified international union be denied participation as a signatory to the contract. Both these conditions to bargaining were illegal, the Supreme Court ruled. In the following years, other issues have also been tested by the mandatory-permissive standard. A union may not insist that an employer contribute to an industry promotion fund, nor may an employer insist that a union provide a performance bond assuring that it will abide by its collective agreement, for example. These subjects have been held to be too remote from the central concerns of the Act to require either party to negotiate about them.

In 1971, the Court rejected the Board's finding that an employer must bargain with a union over benefits for employees who have retired from employment. The Board ruled in this case, *Pittsburgh Plate Glass Company,* that retired employees remained employees within the meaning of the Labor Act, at least with respect to retirement benefits that arose out of collective bargaining. Moreover, the Board decided that the subject of benefits for retired employees was one of vital and immediate concern to active employees. The Supreme Court disagreed with both conclusions. In fact, many employers and unions bargained about this subject before the Board's decision and continue to do so now, although they are not required to do so.

Unquestionably, the most important and controversial decision concerning the subject matter of bargaining is the 1964 decision of the Supreme Court in the *Fibreboard Paper Products Corporation* case. This case, which has been the subject of one book-length study and innumerable articles, dealt with the issue of subcontracting bargaining-unit work. The employer subcontracted janitorial maintenance work of his plant to an outside firm, replacing his employees with those of an outsider who did substantially identical work on the employer's premises. The Board ruled that the decision to subcontract was embraced by the bargaining obligation of the Labor Act, because it vitally affected the jobs of replaced employees. Before taking the subcontracting action, therefore, the employer should have notified the union and given it an opportunity to bargain about the desirability of subcontracting and rearrangements that might mitigate the need for subcontracting. Management argued that subcontracting is a fundamental managerial prerogative that need not be submitted to bargaining. The Supreme Court, however, agreed with the Board. In a unanimous decision the Court commented:

> One of the primary purposes of the act is to promote the peaceful settlement of industrial disputes by subjecting labor-management controversies to the mediatory influence of negotiation. The act was framed with an awareness that refusals to confer and negotiate had been one of the most prolific causes of industrial strife. . . . To hold, as the Board has done, that contracting out is a mandatory subject of collective bargaining would promote the fundamental purpose of the act by bringing

a problem of vital concern to labor and management within the framework established by Congress as most conducive to industrial peace.

The *Fibreboard* principle has been applied to a host of other issues involving major managerial changes that have a direct and important impact on employees and work opportunities in the bargaining unit. Among these are major technological changes, plant removal and relocation, reorganization of work arrangements, and the like. The *Fibreboard* decision does not require an employer to forgo undertaking any of these actions forever; it merely requires that, before they are taken, the representative of affected employees be given notice and an opportunity to bargain about them. If the parties reach an impasse in negotiations over these subjects, the employer is free to take such contemplated actions with impunity, as far as the NLRB is concerned.

Fibreboard brought a storm of controversy and criticism on the Board's head. Leading management spokesmen condemned the decision as incompatible with the efficient and profitable management of enterprise. One management attorney charged that *Fibreboard* was the importation into American labor relations of the German notion of "co-determination," under which workers sit on the governing boards of German enterprises and participate in managerial decision-making. *The Wall Street Journal* kept its editorial writers busy dreaming up new epithets to hurl at the Board and the Supreme Court. And during the Ervin committee hearings in 1968 the one issue on which all management witnesses agreed was their dislike of *Fibreboard*.

There is currently a discernible pause, if not a retreat, in the Board's application of the *Fibreboard* principle. Perhaps this is a reaction to the employers' cries of anguish. More probably it is in response to the refusal of a number of appellate courts to enforce earlier Board decisions on plant closings or removals. The new demarcation line appears to be that employer decisions concerning major shifts in a business, product design, the commitment or withdrawal of capital, and the like are, in the words of Justice Potter Stewart, "at the core of entrepreneurial control," and they should not be and are not subject to the bargaining obligation.

In contrast to the continuing controversy over the scope of the "decision-bargaining" obligation, however, there is general acceptance by the reviewing courts of the Board's rulings that the Act requires employers to bargain at least over the *effects* of such business shifts on employees' jobs and working conditions.

With historical detachment, it is possible both to understand the concern of the management community over the *Fibreboard* decision and, at the same time, to believe that the concern and criticisms were highly exaggerated. In fact, the Board has applied the principle rather cautiously, and few employers have demonstrably suffered any real impairment of managerial freedom of action. Many employers have totally avoided the impact of *Fibreboard* by negotiating clauses that explicitly protect management's sole right to make all decisions concerning subcontracting, technological change, and other issues without consulting with the union, and it is perfectly legal to negotiate such protective clauses. Other employers have, indeed, been required to bargain about subcontracting and related issues with unions, but, after bargaining, they have been free to take these actions without restraint. Still others have bargained about these issues with unions and have found, to their surprise, perhaps, that unions have made accommodations and suggestions that have aided management and simultaneously protected the job interests of employees.

Successor Employers

Since World War II, there has been an unprecedented level of corporate mergers, acquisitions, and other rearrangements of ownership and control of business entities. The ultimate expression of this trend is the conglomerate business. Each such change or rearrangement of ownership or management has a significant impact on collective bargaining relationships, which the Board has dealt with in a variety of contexts.

In 1972, one major aspect of the Board's work in this area reached the Supreme Court in the *Burns International Security Services* case. For five years, the Wackenhut Corporation had provided guard services for a plant in California. In February, 1967, Wackenhut's employees selected a union as their bargaining agent in an NLRB election, and, two months later, Wackenhut and the union signed a 3-year collective agreement. Several months after that, in July, 1967, Wackenhut lost its contract to provide guard services at this plant, and a new guard service, Burns, took over. Burns employed forty-two employees as guards at this plant, twenty-seven of whom had previously been employed by Wackenhut.

On assuming management of the guard service, Burns refused to recognize the union and declined the union's request to honor the 3-year contract that had been recently concluded with Wackenhut, the predecessor employer. Thereupon, the union filed unfair labor practice charges with the Board. Among other things, the union alleged that Burns violated Section 8(a)(5)'s bargaining obligation both by its refusal to recognize the union as bargaining agent for its forty-two employees and by its refusal to live up to the existing 3-year contract with Wackenhut.

The Board ruled in the union's favor. Because a substantial majority of those whom Burns had hired at this plant were Wackenhut's guards, the Board reasoned that the union continued to be the majority representative of employees. And, based on the fact that the bargaining unit had not significantly changed when Burns became the operator of the guard service, and that Burns was informed about the 3-year contract when it took over from Wackenhut, the Board ruled that Burns was also obligated to honor the contract. On the first issue, the Supreme Court agreed with the Board, but it disagreed on the second.

When a new employer purchases or otherwise acquires an existing business and does not substantially change its method of operation, the new employer must continue to recognize the bargaining status of the union that represents employees, the Supreme Court ruled. In other words, a mere change of technical ownership or management does not upset established representation rights under the Labor Act; these are rights of employees that are not extinguished by ownership changes, as long as the employees remain together in the original bargaining unit.

But the Supreme Court disagreed that Burns was also obligated to honor the contract signed with its precedessor, Wackenhut. The Court decided that both the union and the successor employer were free to negotiate a totally new contract but that neither was bound by the Wackenhut contract. The Board had emphasized the importance of achieving industrial stability through enforcement of existing contractual obligations. The Supreme Court, however, stressed the Section 8(d) provision that good faith bargaining does not require either party to make concessions and the legal principle derived from it— that the Board has no authority to compel a party to accept any substantial contract provision—as the basis for its ruling that the successor had no duty to assume the contract of its predecessor.

Refusal to Bargain with a Majority Union

One of the most controversial of the Board's rulings is the *Joy Silk* doctrine. Essentially, an employer who commits substantial unfair labor practices during an organizing campaign, and thereby destroys the union's majority before an election can be conducted, will be ordered under this doctrine to recognize and bargain with the union, even if the union later loses the election. *Joy Silk* has had a complex legal history that culminated in a 1969 decision of the Supreme Court, in the *Gissel Packing Company* case, approving the ruling.

Unions customarily attempt to organize employees by requesting them to sign so-called authorization cards, which designate the union as the signer's exclusive bargaining agent. If a union has persuaded a majority of the employees in an appropriate unit to sign such cards, and, thereafter, the employer engages in unfair labor practices, what are likely to be the results? The union might win the election in any event. Or, in some instances, the employer's unfair labor practices may cause the union to lose the majority it had before the election by frightening and coercing employees. Of course, the Board could always conduct another election, but, in certain instances, the Board believes, it would be futile to conduct a second election, because of the continuing effects of the unfair labor practices. In order to protect employees' statutory rights and to prevent employers from enjoying the fruits of their illegal acts, the Board requires the employer to recognize and bargain with the union that enjoyed majority status through authorization cards before the unfair labor practices were committed by the employer.

This doctrine is hedged by a number of conditions: First, the union must prove that a majority of employees in the unit voluntarily signed authorization cards designating the union as their bargaining agent. Second, the employer's unfair labor practices must have been sufficiently serious to warrant setting an election aside and also sufficiently serious to justify imposition of a bargaining-order remedy. Third, the Board must be satisfied that there is no likelihood that a second election could be conducted without being tainted by lingering effects of the employer's illegal acts.

SECONDARY BOYCOTTS

The union secondary boycott has been the most complex and persistent form of illegal union conduct under the Labor Act. Congress has had enormous difficulty defining secondary boycotts in statutory language, and many cases have been decided by the Supreme Court.

A secondary boycott is essentially an economic strategy in which a union that has a labor dispute with one employer—usually called the "primary" employer—attempts to put various kinds of pressure on other employers—called "neutral" or "secondary" employers—to stop doing business with the primary one. In a classic example of a secondary boycott Union A calls a strike at a shoe factory and places picket lines around it. In order to prevent the factory from getting raw materials, Union A sends a picket line to the tannery that supplies leather to the struck employer. Union B, which represents the employees of the tannery, urges its members to respect the picket line at the tannery. In order to get its own employees back to work, the tannery will stop sending leather to the struck shoe factory. Union A then sends its pickets to shoe stores that sell shoes made by the struck factory. Union C, which represents employees of the shoe stores, urges its members to respect the picket lines in front of their stores. Again, in order to get their own employees back to work, the shoe stores will agree to stop selling shoes made at the factory. As a result, the struck factory has been deprived of raw materials to manufacture shoes and has lost its sources of retail distribution. It is being economically strangled, and it can only break the strangle hold by coming to an agreement with Union A.

Congress sought to confine the scope of labor disputes and to limit union economic power by declaring it an unfair labor practice for a union to pressure neutral or secondary employers in order to compel the primary employer to reach an agreement with his own employees. In the example above, it would be illegal for Union A to place its pickets either at the tannery or at the retail stores.

The secondary-boycott provisions of the Taft-Hartley Act were so complex and byzantine that unions quickly found a number of loopholes. In the 1959 Landrum-Griffin Amendments, Congress sought to close these loopholes in a variety of ways. The Board and courts are still engaged in the decades-old effort to define the legitimate scope of labor disputes within the framework of Congress's extraordinarily vague and uncertain policy guidelines.

RACE AND SEX DISCRIMINATION

The NLRB has dealt with issues of race discrimination in labor relations for many years. Historically, for example, it has revoked the certification of unions that in collective bargaining discriminate against employees on the basis of race.

In recent years, the reach of the Labor Act has been tested by cases that question whether it is an unfair labor practice for a union or employer to discriminate against an employee because of race or sex.

In the *Miranda* and *Hughes Tool* cases in 1963 and 1964, a Board majority ruled that such arbitrary and invidious discrimination by a *union* is an unfair labor practice. It relied on earlier court decisions that, as the Act [Section 9(a)] confers upon a union chosen by a majority the exclusive right to represent *all* employees in the bargaining unit, the union has a duty to represent all *fairly*. Breach of that duty, the Board held, restrains employees in the exercise of their Section 7 rights and tends to encourage union fealty, in violation of Sections 8(b) (1) (A) and 8(b) 2. Although the majority did not expressly rule on the question, in the Supreme Court's decision in *Vaca* v. *Sipes* in 1967, several justices approved the doctrine; and the Board through various membership changes has not departed from it, despite a somewhat mixed reception in the courts of appeals.

In a different context—a case by a union against an employer refusing to bargain—a court of appeals recently held that a union's racial discrimination, if proved, is a ground for denying it the customary Board bargaining order against the employer.

Cases involving *employer* racial discrimination, however, have had a different history. Here the union's duty of fair representation, first articulated by the courts, does not come into play. In a well-known case, the Board concluded that employer race discrimination per se is not illegal under the Labor Act, reasoning that Congress simply did not intend the NLRB to deal with problems of racial discrimination. Instead, Congress entrusted primary responsibility to the Equal Employment Opportunity Commission under the Civil Rights Act of 1964 to deal with employment-related race discrimination. In a very recent case, the NLRB reached the same conclusion with respect to discrimination in employment based on sex. At least one court of appeals has reached an opposite conclusion concerning an employer's racial discrimination.

Surprisingly, the volume of charges seeking to test and activate the Board's authority in this area has not been great. The delays in other forums and the probing of the courts may change this picture in the future.

THE NLRB AND ARBITRATION

There has been a long-standing controversy over how the Board should process cases where the alleged unfair labor practices involve conduct that may also be a breach of a collective bargaining contract in which the union and employer have agreed on an arbitration procedure to resolve disputes under the contract. Section 10(a) of the law asserts the primacy of the Board's jurisdiction, regardless of parties' agreements, but Section 203(d) affirms that final adjustment by agreed-upon methods is "the desirable method" for settling grievance disputes under contracts. With the Act thus looking in both directions, the Board has had to draw the lines when these situations of overlapping jurisdiction are laid before it.

For many years, two general approaches have been followed: If the grievance-arbitration process has been started, the regional office will defer action until its completion. If a party still claims his rights under the Act after an arbitration award is rendered, the Board will examine the merits of the case but "defer" to the award, if all parties had clearly agreed to arbitration, if the proceedings were fair and regular, and if the award is not "repugnant" to the law, the principles derived from the *Spielberg* case.

Now, in its furthest departure from past practice, in 1971, a majority of the Board in the *Collyer* case decided, with qualifications not amenable to summary here, that henceforth when the issues raised in the unfair labor practice case are cognizable under the parties' arbitration procedures, even though neither party has invoked them, the Board will defer its consideration of the case until after the parties have traveled the arbitration road. If then requested, it will test the conduct complained against and the arbitration award by the principles noted above. Although applied most frequently in cases alleging violations of an employer's duty to bargain, the principle has also governed the Board's decisions in a broad range of other cases. The first court of appeals to review the Board's decision has approved it, and there has long been strong judicial support for arbitration. The dissenters on the Board have persisted, however, in asserting that the Board has unwisely limited its powers to remedy statutory violations, and it may require the elucidating processes of considerable litigation to determine finally the validity and reach of this *Collyer* principle.

There is no doubt of the value of encouraging parties to live by the voluntary system they have created to resolve their disputes and to utilize the tremendous assets of experienced arbitrators. In the vast majority of grievance cases, they now do this. But there is equally no doubt of the superiority of the Board's investigative processes and experience with statutory issues, and the burden of mounting arbitration costs on some parties is clear. Whether one believes the Board should have adopted its rather sweeping "exhaustion of contract remedies" principle or should allow the parties in a particular case to choose their forum will depend largely on how one balances the foregoing values.

IX

The NLRB and the Future
of Labor Relations

In personnel and appropriations, the Board has always been one of the smallest agencies in the federal galaxy. Its members and general counsel do not sit in the President's Cabinet, and their names have rarely been recognizable to the general public.

Although an occasional NLRB decision makes headlines, most of its daily work—conducting elections and processing unfair labor practice charges—is performed in efficient obscurity, immediately important only to the parties affected.

THE CONTRIBUTION OF THE NLRB

From the day of its official birth on July 5, 1935, the Board has been the cutting edge of social reform and fair treatment at industrial society's most vital spot, the workplace. In his monumental study of administrative agencies, Louis Jaffe of the Harvard Law School wrote:

> If we use the hopes of their proponents as the measure . . . the National Labor Relations Board and the Securities and Exchange Commission . . . have been successful. They have,

in their fields, made remarkable contributions to the reorientation of American society. They are only two evidences of a legislative and administrative movement which has profoundly changed our society, a change which can be set down beside the English Reform Movement of the Nineteenth Century as one of the greatest historical jobs of law-making.

Thirty years after leaving the agency, Judge J. Warren Madden wrote, "The statute as applied has been the most significant legislation of this century. It has brought freedom and dignity to scores of millions of working people, and prosperity to the country."

It is difficult to catalog the precise contribution of the Labor Act and the Board. But the figures alone tell a story of impressive agency achievement. For 1972:

> 41,000 new cases were processed;
> 90 per cent were disposed of in about forty-five days;
> 9,000 elections were conducted;
> 525,000 votes were cast in Board elections;
> 6,400 unfair labor practice cases were settled or adjusted;
> $6.5 million were distributed in back pay to 6,200 employees;
> 3,500 employees were offered reinstatement—2,500 accepted;
> in 1,675 cases collective bargaining was begun;
> in 750 cases picketing was ended;
> in 320 cases work stoppages were ended;
> 3,400 violation notices were posted;
> 1,400 Board decisions in contested cases were issued;
> 361 proceedings were decided by U.S. courts of appeals.

This is a picture of widespread protection of employee and employer rights, of many potential sources of industrial conflict, particularly at the growing edge of organization, yielding to orderly and fair processes.

More importantly, on the foundation of legal protections

provided by this Act and other similar federal and state laws and orders, employees and employers have erected the American structure of collective bargaining relationships. This structure orders the working lives of an estimated 23 million persons directly and countless millions more indirectly. It has brought a greater measure of due process and justice to the workplace. It has given to individual workers a more effective voice in shaping the conditions and contours of their working lives. It has fostered greater stability in industrial operations. And in these later years the laws and the bargaining structure are also giving needed protections to individuals in their job rights against unlawful discriminations by some powerful union institutions.

It does not belittle the enormous contributions of the labor and management groups who have created and who operate this system to point out the essential supportive role that the law plays.

Despite this experience and these successes, however, there is no respite for the NLRB. The steady rise in case intake, the arrant opposition to the law, the delays in litigated cases, and the shortcomings in Board remedies, which we review in this chapter, are also part of the picture. They underline the need for renewed measures to redeem the promises of the Act.

Many regulatory agencies have become so closely identified with the parties they were created to regulate that their dedication to the public interest has been properly challenged. Some have been so intimidated by the industries they regulate, or by Congress or the White House, that they lack the will to respond to the public's needs. The NLRB, for a variety of reasons, has never ceased to be in the center of controversy between labor and management and has, thus, been under constant pressure to examine its statutory responsibilities in the light of social and economic change. Its role does not permit it the doubtful luxury of a quiet and comfortable relationship with those whose conduct it must monitor. The Board operates almost entirely in a fishbowl atmosphere, and this must account for some of its vitality: All of its unfair labor practice decisions are subject to judicial review, and many of its representation decisions are ultimately reviewed in the courts, when they constitute part of an unfair labor practice proceeding.

The NLRB, like other agencies, is certainly not free from the vicissitudes of political change. As indicated in earlier chapters, the Board's leadership and, consequently, its attitudes have altered from decade to decade and from President to President. No less is true of the Supreme Court, however, whose own change in membership has historically produced significant shifts in Constitutional philosophy.

When the New Deal created regulatory agencies in large numbers in the 1930's, the prevailing view of the times was that such agencies should be wholly above partisan politics. They should, it was argued, provide a consistent and continuous administration of congressional laws without regard to the current occupant in the White House. In recent decades political theorists have not only come to recognize that this earlier notion was largely unrealistic; they have come to appreciate that administrative agencies may serve the public interest best when they respond to changes in national political sentiment reflected in Presidential elections.

To practiced observers of the Board's work, however, the continuity of its administration—despite changes of leadership and philosophy—has been remarkably strong. It has not been spared the appointment of occasional partisans and "wreckers" to its important offices, but most of its members and staff have, for four decades, been persons of integrity and commitment to the values of the statute.

Although one might wish that labor and management could find common ground in accepting both the statutory rules that Congress has laid down in the Labor Act and the Board's role as impartial arbiter of those rules, there is little evidence that partisan bickering and hostility will soon disappear. The Board's environment has always been one of unrelenting controversy; that seems unlikely to change.

Those who are not partisans, however, have little difficulty appreciating that the Board has not only survived but has performed honorably and effectively in carrying out Congress's will in the face of controversy and hostility. The Board, it has been observed, is Congress's lightning rod for statutory policies that have never been accepted by large parts of the labor-management community.

During the 1960's, nearly 10 million public employees began the process of organizing for collective bargaining with their federal, state, and local governmental employers. These employees are not covered by the terms of the Labor Act. Instead, their right to organize and engage in bargaining is governed by executive orders, state statutes, and local ordinances. With remarkable consistency, virtually every state and city that has faced the problem of establishing a new framework for collective bargaining for government employees has adopted the Labor Act and the NLRB as its model. In this sense, the Board's work is being extended to millions of workers who have no direct contact whatever with it.

In England, whose troubled industrial-relations system has caused it to search for more effective solutions, a new Industrial Relations Act passed by Parliament in 1971 is also patterned on the National Labor Relations Act.

These are but a few evidences that the Board and the statute it administers have proved their worth through the acid tests of history.

PROPOSALS TO RESTRUCTURE THE BOARD

For several decades, proposals to reorganize or abolish the Board have received considerable attention. Across the spectrum of informed opinion, there is agreement that the Board should be more intelligently structured. Those who are sympathetic to the policies of the Labor Act advocate reforms to make the Board's work more efficient. Those who are unsympathetic prefer changes to make the Board's work more cumbersome and legalistic. The result has been a congressional standoff.

In 1950, Congress, enmeshed in the ferocious politics following the enactment of Taft-Hartley, turned down President Truman's proposal to abolish the office of the independent general counsel and to transfer his powers to the NLRB Chairman. In 1959, the Landrum-Griffin Act authorized the NLRB to delegate its decision-making powers in representation cases to its thirty-one regional directors. The Board implemented this authority by delegation rules in 1961, and the results have been universally applauded. President Kennedy introduced some Board reforms in Congress in 1961. Reorganization Plan No. 5 would have accorded greater finality to the decisions of administrative law judges (then called trial examiners), particularly with respect to findings of fact, relieving the Board of the heavy burden of reviewing hundreds of routine unfair labor practice cases each year. This proposal had the agency's support and the endorsement of most nonpartisan observers, but it was voted down in the House. James Landis, the late dean of the Harvard Law School and President Kennedy's adviser on administrative agencies, attributed Congress's refusal to approve the plan "to one cause, namely the absence of any desire on the part of conservative elements of the Congress to make the [Labor Act] a workable act."

In the years since the defeat of Plan No. 5, new support has rallied to the proposal to make administrative law judges' findings more final in routine, factual cases. The Administrative Conference of the United States has endorsed it, as have individual members of the Board and respected observers in and out of government.

Senator John Tower of Texas has introduced legislation that would strip the Board of its authority to decide unfair labor practice cases and transfer that authority to the several hundred U.S. district court judges. This proposal is vigorously opposed by most nonpartisan authorities in the labor-law field as one calculated to undermine the policies of the Labor

Act by delaying its operation interminably. Such a reorganization would treat unfair labor practice cases like other civil cases and destroy the uniformity of administration that can be achieved only by a single judicial body.

Senator Robert Griffin of Michigan has introduced legislation to convert the Board into a federal labor court whose judges sit in several sections of the country. While the Griffin proposal would not destroy the national character of the agency, the specifics of that plan would compound existing administrative problems that delay the final disposition of cases.

That Congress's political configuration has prevented an objective, nonpartisan approach to the Board's need for more streamlined procedures is characteristic of its historic approach to all labor-relations problems. The standoff, however, is no less inexcusable for this explanation. With each passing year, the Board's case load seems inexorably to grow and grow. The five Board members must allocate their time between large numbers of routine, essentially factual cases and those cases that raise issues of transcendent importance to the industrial-relations system. Too often, the Board simply lacks the time to consider important issues fully; too often, the Board, absorbed as it is with the pressing details of the moment, lacks the time to plan for the future; too often, routine cases that should be speeded through the Board to provide prompt protection to parties whose rights have been violated become stalled in the multilevel system of review.

NLRB Chairman Edward B. Miller has repeatedly sounded the alarm to the labor-management community and to Congress about the Board's cumbersome processes and the need for sensible reorganization. In February, 1972, he wrote an article for the magazine of the U.S. Chamber of Commerce— itself a traditional foe of Plan No. 5 and other internal reorganization plans—that concludes with an expression of surprise that the Board's administrative apparatus works as well as it does:

The five-man Board in Washington *is* handling those 1,200-plus cases a year in a surprisingly creditable way. And thanks to a first-class field organization over 30,000 additional cases are disposed of by locally achieved settlements, withdrawals, or other expeditious means—and this latter astronomic number within a median time of 45 days, which is an amazingly good record. . . .

The processes of democracy are slow and often cumbersome. But reforms in our institutions can [be] and have been achieved through those processes when the public demands reform, and when the need is sufficiently obvious that even distrustful opposing forces realize that a procedural reform must be undertaken jointly, and not as part of substantive law changes on which they will doubtless continue to differ.

By mid-1973, as Chairman Miller warned the Labor Law Section of the American Bar Association, the Board's annual decisional output had risen above 1,400, and the agency's total case intake had passed the 40,000 level. Something has to give.

THE INADEQUACY OF THE BOARD'S REMEDIES

Nonpartisan observers agree that statutory remedies for serious unfair labor practices are woefully inadequate. Particular concern has been focused on discriminatory discharges and the refusal to bargain in good faith over first contracts.

When an employee is discharged for illegal reasons, he may be required to wait two years or more, before the unfair labor practice procedures of the Act—the investigation, trial, appeal to the Board, and appeal to the courts—have been completed. During this waiting period, he receives no compensation from his employer, and often he is barred from unemployment compensation benefits under state law. If he is unable to find other employment—and such cases are not unusual—his family situation might become desperate. Moreover, because discriminatory discharges often occur during the course of organizing campaigns, the effect may be to radiate fear throughout a plant and undermine the free choice of employees. And, when the litigation is over, the maximum remedy presently available under the law is reinstatement with back pay with interest, from which interim earnings must be deducted. The reinstatement-with-back-pay remedy is such an inconsequential price to pay for acts of discrimination that there are, doubtless, some employers who find it to their advantage to violate the law.

The Board's remedial powers are inadequate to deal with conscious and strategic acts of discrimination. While the Board might mitigate the harsh consequences of protracted delays in discharge cases by seeking interim injunctions under Section 10(j), this alternative is administratively impractical to cope with the hundreds of such cases that are filed each year. In fiscal year 1972, the Board received over 11,000 charges of employer discrimination of various types and nearly 2,000 charges of union discrimination. Not all of these were discharge cases, of course, nor did all of them have merit.

In 1967, the Special Subcommittee on Labor of the House of Representatives, under the leadership of Representative Frank Thompson, Jr., held hearings on a bill that would have strengthened the Board's statutory remedial power in discrimination cases by several devices. Administrative law judges' decisions in routine cases would have been accorded greater finality, thereby minimizing the effects of delay. The federal courts of appeals would also have been authorized to direct that a discharged employee be reinstated pending judicial review, if an administrative law judge had first found that his discharge was illegal. Finally, a federal loan fund would have been created for employees, while they await the outcome of litigation.

The same House committee returned to these issues in 1971, in hearings on H.R. 7152. This bill would have amended the Act to authorize dischargees to file civil suits for treble damages, plus costs and attorney's fees. It would also have enabled the Board to delegate greater finality to administrative law judges' unfair labor practice decisions, subject to discretionary Board review. Finally, H.R. 7152 provided for the Board the expedited access to court enforcement now available to other major administrative agencies. Although these, as well as many other imaginative proposals, deserve serious consideration, there is no indication that Congress will view this entire problem with any urgency in the near future. Even procedural reforms to reduce delays and speed Board and court enforcement have gotten submerged in the wary search for partisan advantage.

A second area in which the Board's remedial powers are grossly inadequate is that of illegal refusals to bargain over first contracts. This is an exceedingly complex problem, and it has received much attention from the Board, the courts, scholars, and practitioners. In essence, the problem is this: Immediately after a union wins a certification election and receives formal certification, it is entitled to act as the bargaining agent of employees. The employer, however, may challenge the validity of the certification by refusing to bargain with the union. The union must then initiate a refusal-to-bargain proceeding under Section 8(a) (5). If this litigation is carried through its many possible steps, including full judicial review, a period of years may elapse before the employer is ultimately directed to go to the bargaining table. At this point, both experience and statistical data demonstrate that the passage of time will have so eroded the union's support in the bargaining unit—through employee turnover and employee frustration—that the likelihood of the union's actually concluding a contract with the employer is greatly diminished. To put it more directly, the longer the employer delays getting to the bargaining table with a certified union, the less likely that union is to negotiate any contract at all. Moreover, during the intervening period, the employees have lost the benefits of representation to which they were legally entitled— the tangible economic gains that ordinarily attend the collective bargaining agreement and the incalculable values of day-to-day representation in the workplace.

In terms of Congress's clear policy of encouraging good faith bargaining between an employer and the duly selected agent of employees, this result is unacceptable; it mocks congressional policy by depriving employees of rights they are entitled to enjoy. As long ago as 1960, an advisory panel under the chairmanship of Archibald Cox of Harvard University reported to the Senate Labor Committee:

> [A] major weakness in the . . . law is the long delay in contested NLRB proceedings. . . . Strikes may occur, the employer's business may be heavily damaged, or the union may wither and die. . . . In labor-management relations justice delayed is often justice denied. A remedy granted more than two years after the event will bear little relation to the human situation which gave rise to the need for Government intervention.

Several federal courts of appeals, including those of the District of Columbia and the First Circuit, have expressed concern that some parties engage in protracted delays through litigation for strategic reasons related to a desire to weaken, if not destroy, a newly certified union.

In recent years, the NLRB has significantly strengthened its remedies in these cases. For example, in one "clear and flagrant" case, it has ordered an employer to pay all expenses of litigation. However, the Board has held that it lacks the statutory power to make employees "whole" for loss of the opportunity to have bargained during the months and years that litigation—often frivolous litigation—has proceeded. This problem is also one that might be resolved more satisfactorily, if the Board's procedures were streamlined to permit faster disposition of routine cases.

Of course, no one takes the position that employers and unions should be deprived of reasonable and full opportunities to defend themselves against charges of illegal conduct. No one has proposed that respondents should be deprived of the right to judicial review of Board orders in cases that raise important issues of law. The question is whether the remedies of the law should not be strengthened, so that parties who invade the rights of employees will not profit from their violations by dint of the corrosive effects of litigation delays.

Great credit is due the Chairman, the general counsel, and their staffs in Washington and in the field offices for their incessant and, in some respects, remarkably successful efforts to reduce these delays. The time lapse from Board decisions to court enforcement has been cut almost in half. But with the rising tide of cases flooding the agency, a determined litigant still holds off the final order far too long.

There is an old maxim in Anglo-American law that for every legal wrong there is a legal remedy. In many instances, wrongs committed under the National Labor Relations Act are remedied either so late or so inadequately that statutory rights have been tragically undermined. It is easy to point a finger of accusation at Congress, which has neglected to ensure that its statutory policies are effectively supported. Congress has not acted, in the face of clear need, to grant adequate remedial authority to be used in suitable cases. But responsibility lies in no small measure with the labor-management community and the organized labor-relations bar for their failure to join in demanding that the Labor Act's procedures be made more expeditious and its remedies more satisfactory.

THOUGHTS OF THE FUTURE

The state of labor-management relations in America of the 1970's would be unrecognizable to the proponents of the Wagner Act of 1935. Collective bargaining has taken hold in virtually every major industry in the nation, most recently among millions of public employees. Corporations and unions that only a generation ago solved their problems with violence now solve them at the bargaining table. Workers who were voiceless in dealing with their working lives have found peaceful, rational, and orderly ways to make their voices heard and respected. To the extent that the Labor Act and the NLRB have contributed to this humane revolution in the workplace, they have been successful.

But there is a dark side of the balance sheet; violations of statutory rights of employees continue at record levels by employers and unions. There are giant corporations and powerful unions that show by their deeds that they are not reconciled to the labor laws of the land. There are glaring deficiencies in the procedures and remedies of the statute that urgently need congressional attention. This probably cannot be expected, however, until the labor and management communities to which Congress is sensitive develop a new consensus about the content and direction of American labor policy.

Appendix A
Career Opportunities with the
National Labor Relations Board

For four decades, young people have gravitated toward the National Labor Relations Board in search of employment, and for good reason. The work of this agency offers opportunities that appeal greatly to those beginning professional careers: the opportunity to play a valuable role in the interesting, often dramatic, field of labor relations; the opportunity to assume responsibility for carrying out congressional policies in an agency that is still small enough to appreciate the contributions of individual staff members; and, last, but perhaps most important, the opportunity to express one's idealism in the achievement of fair and decent treatment for workers in our complex industrial society.

Because of its popularity, the NLRB has usually had relatively few openings for its professional positions, and it has, therefore, chosen carefully from among many qualified applicants. This is true both of the Washington offices of the Board and the general counsel and of the thirty-one field offices.

In Washington, the agency employs large numbers of lawyers and clerical workers and a small number of other professionals. The lawyers work as legal assistants to the five members of the Board, as personal staff members, and in all of the specialized offices of the general counsel. In the field offices, the agency employs an approximately equal number of lawyers and field examiners, who have the most direct contact with employees, unions, and employers; in this sense, their work is particularly challenging. By contrast, those who work in the Washington offices of the agency tend to deal with policy and decisional problems or with appellate litigation.

For those with a sense of the importance and drama in the agency's work, the Board's field offices offer rich variety. Lawyers and examiners conduct elections, investigate unfair labor practice charges, and preside over representation hearings. Field attorneys prosecute unfair labor practice cases before administrative law judges.

A wag once said that the NLRB is the finest graduate school of labor relations in the country. By this, he meant that many young people, particularly young lawyers, begin their professional careers with the NLRB and, after several years, leave to work for private employers and unions as partisan advocates. The Board has, in fact, served as a postgraduate training school for many of the country's leading labor-relations specialists. Until recently, government salaries were less attractive than those in the private sector, but today government salaries are quite competitive. One hopes that the "brain drain" away from government service might, therefore, be discouraged.

For those who devote their entire careers to the agency, there are opportunities for promotion to positions of high responsibility and prestige. Many of the agency's administrative law judges, for example, are career attorneys; this is equally true of the agency's regional directors and division heads.

Although the NLRB is an especially attractive agency to young people who wish to make a career in the labor field, other federal agencies also offer diverse opportunities to be involved in labor-management relations—principally the Department of Labor, the Equal Employment Opportunity Commission, the Federal Mediation and Conciliation Service, and the National Mediation Board.

The NLRB is not a place for labor or management partisans, although it has had its share of both in its history. It is, rather, a place for men and women who have a sense of balance, fairness, and impartiality, who strive—in the words of the late Benjamin M. Selekman of Harvard—for the "possibilities of making cooperation in industry something as active, exacting, and tangibly rewarding as the traditional fight for the causes and demands in which men believe."

Appendix B
Statistical Data

TABLE B-1. Case Intake Experience
(Cases Filed, 1958–72)

Fiscal Year	Unfair Labor Practice Cases	Representation Cases	Union De-authorizations	Amendments of Certification	Unit Clarifications	Total
1958	9,260	7,399	89	—	—	16,748
1959	12,239	9,347	47	—	—	21,633
1960	11,357	10,130	40	—	—	21,527
1961	12,132	10,508	51	—	—	22,691
1962	13,479	11,286	83	—	—	24,848
1963	14,166	11,116	89	—	—	25,371
1964	15,620	11,685	98	—	—	27,403
1965	15,800	11,989	106	45	85	28,025
1966	15,933	12,620	137	124	179	28,993
1967	17,040	12,957	125	86	217	30,425
Ten-Year Period	137,026	109,037	865	255	481	247,664
1968	17,816	12,307	152	194	236	30,705
1969	18,651	12,107	173	134	238	31,303
1970	21,038	12,077	158	107	201	33,581
1971	23,770	12,965	168	86	223	37,212
1972	26,852	13,711	172	83	221	41,039

— = Not Applicable

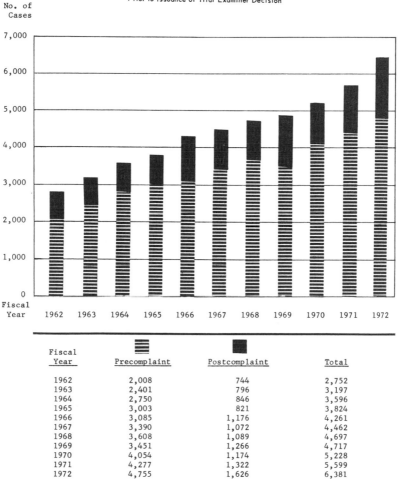

Chart B-I.
UNFAIR LABOR PRACTICE CASES SETTLED.

TABLE B-2
Remedial Action Taken in Unfair Labor Practice Cases Closed (Fiscal Years 1958–72)

						Number of Cases				
Fiscal Year	Total Number of Cases Closed	Notice Posted	Recognition or Other Assistance Withdrawn	Employer Dominated Union Disestablished	Employees Placed on Preferential Hiring List	Collective Bargaining Began	Picketing Ended	Work Stoppage Ended	Employees Offered Reinstatement	Back-pay Was Distributed
1958	7,289	1,060	114	23	39	128	—	—	—	—
1959	11,465	1,529	267	29	49	168	—	—	—	—
1960	11,924	2,299	248	33	90	315	—	—	—	—
1961	12,526	2,791	203	22	96	371	—	—	—	—
1962	13,319	2,554	150	29	72	526	—	—	—	—
1963	13,605	2,468	110	45	133	673	—	—	—	—
1964	15,074	2,680	113	32	146	986	332	114	1,161	1,073
1965	15,219	2,688	90	37	152	1,175	451	184	1,122	1,467
1966	15,587	2,766	104	44	90	1,229	526	222	1,177	1,222
1967	16,360	2,805	76	50	92	1,451	606	261	1,184	1,641
1968	17,777	2,861	89	20	122	1,531	665	296	1,281	1,726
1969	18,939	2,363	62	27	131	1,388	733	270	1,405	1,679
1970	19,851	3,003	102	37	110	1,657	676	349	952	1,660
1971	23,840	3,253	67	17	115	1,620	755	349	1,248	1,856
1972	25,555	3,488	119	37	143	1,673	746	323	1,029	1,679

[a] Includes thirty-two West Coast trucking industry cases involving 41,200 workers.

Number of Employees

Fiscal Year	Offered Reinstatement	Accepted Reinstatement	Receiving Backpay		Amount Recovered	
			From Either Employer or Union	From Both Employer and Union	Backpay	Fees, Dues, and Fines
1958	1,067	821	1,244	124	$761,933	$4,842
1959	42,078a	41,890	1,197	324	900,110	10,565
1960	1,885	1,351	2,923	187	1,139,810	11,690
1961	2,650	2,377	3,476	152	1,685,750	55,562
1962	2,455	2,100	3,126	97	1,751,910	39,460
1963	3,478	2,297	6,836	54	2,749,151	36,890
1964	4,044	3,004	5,124	18	3,001,630	55,550
1965	5,875	5,081	4,591	53	2,782,360	25,420
1966	6,187	4,624	15,418	48	8,911,040	63,580
1967	4,274	3,436	13,936	136	3,248,850	37,610
1968	3,107	2,061	6,258	16	3,189,340	38,660
1969	3,748	2,726	6,213	12	4,370,430	156,890
1970	3,779	2,723	6,806	27	3,749,370	114,170
1971	4,068	2,763	6,738	32	4,594,650	230,925
1972	3,555	2,544	6,093	132	6,448,640	122,050

Proceedings

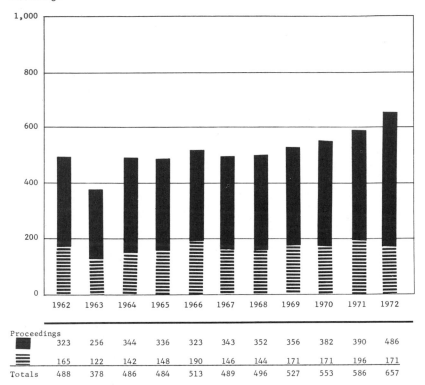

Proceedings

	1962	1963	1964	1965	1966	1967	1968	1969	1970	1971	1972
■	323	256	344	336	323	343	352	356	382	390	486
≡	165	122	142	148	190	146	144	171	171	196	171
Totals	488	378	486	484	513	489	496	527	553	586	657

Chart B-II.
BOARD CASE BACKLOG. Solid bars show unfair labor complaints; striped bars show representation cases.

Bibliography

HISTORICAL MATERIALS

BERNSTEIN, IRVING. *Turbulent Years: A History of the American Worker, 1933–1941*. Boston: Houghton Mifflin, 1969.

GALENSON, WALTER. *The CIO Challenge to the AFL: A History of the American Labor Movement, 1935–1941*. Cambridge: Harvard University Press, 1960.

LEE, R. ALTON. *Truman and Taft-Hartley: A Question of Mandate*. Lexington: University of Kentucky Press, 1966.

MCADAMS, ALAN K. *Power and Politics in Labor Legislation*. New York: Columbia University Press, 1964.

MILLIS, HARRY A., and EMILY CLARK BROWN. *From the Wagner Act to Taft-Hartley*. Chicago: University of Chicago Press, 1950.

"National Labor Relations Board: Silver Anniversary Commemorative Symposium," *George Washington Law Review*, Vol. 29, No. 2, December, 1960, pp. 191–489.

PATTERSON, JAMES T. *Mr. Republican: A Biography of Robert A. Taft*. Boston: Houghton Mifflin, 1972.

RAYBACK, JOSEPH G. *A History of American Labor*. New York: The Free Press, 1966.

ROSENFARB, JOSEPH. *The National Labor Policy and How It Works*. New York: Harper & Brothers, 1940.

SILVERBERG, LOUIS G., ed. *The Wagner Act: After Ten Years*. Washington, D.C.: Bureau of National Affairs, 1945.

LEGAL MATERIALS

GREGORY, CHARLES O. *Labor and the Law*. 2nd rev. ed. New York: Norton, 1961.

MORRIS, CHARLES, ed. *The Developing Labor Law: The Board, the Courts, and the National Labor Relations Act.* Washington, D.C.: Bureau of National Affairs, 1970.

National Labor Relations Board. *Annual Reports,* 1935–72.

———. *Legislative History of the Labor Management and Reporting and Disclosure Act, 1959.* 2 vols. Washington, D.C.: 1960.

———. *Legislative History of the Labor Management Relations Act, 1947.* 2 vols. Washington, D.C.: 1948.

———. *Legislative History of the National Labor Relations Act, 1935.* 2 vols. Washington, D.C.: 1949.

SCHLOSSBERG, STEPHEN I., and FREDERICK E. SHERMAN. *Organizing and the Law.* Washington, D.C.: Bureau of National Affairs, 1971.

SILVERBERG, LOUIS, and KENNETH C. McGUINESS. *How To Take a Case Before the National Labor Relations Board.* 3d ed. Washington, D.C.: Bureau of National Affairs, 1967.

U.S. HOUSE OF REPRESENTATIVES. Committee on Education and Labor. Subcommittee on National Labor Relations Board. *Administration of the Labor Management Relations Act by the NLRB.* Washington, D.C.: September, 1961.

———. Special Subcommittee on Labor. *National Labor Relations Act Remedies: The Unfulfilled Promise.* Washington, D.C.: December, 1968.

U.S. SENATE. Committee on the Judiciary. Subcommittee on Separation of Powers. *Congressional Oversight of Administrative Agencies (National Labor Relations Board).* Washington, D.C. 1970.

WELLINGTON, HARRY H. *Labor and the Legal Process.* New Haven: Yale University Press, 1968.

AMERICAN LABOR RELATIONS IN GENERAL

BOK, DEREK C., and JOHN T. DUNLOP. *Labor and the American Community.* New York: Simon and Schuster, 1970.

CHAMBERLAIN, NEIL W., and DONALD E. CULLEN. *The Labor Sector.* 2d ed. New York: McGraw-Hill, 1971.

COHEN, SANFORD. *Labor in the United States.* 3d ed. Columbus: Merrill, 1970.

DERBER, MILTON. *The American Idea of Industrial Democracy: 1865–1965.* Urbana: University of Illinois Press, 1970.

HEALY, JAMES J., ed. *Creative Collective Bargaining: Meeting Today's Challenge to Labor-Management Relations.* Englewood Cliffs, N.J.: Prentice-Hall, 1965.

INDEPENDENT STUDY GROUP. *The Public Interest in National Labor Policy.* New York: Committee for Economic Development, 1961.

Ross, Philip. *The Government as a Source of Union Power.* Providence: Brown University Press, 1965.

Rowan, Richard, ed. *Readings in Labor Economics and Labor Relations.* Revised ed. Homewood, Ill.: Richard D. Irwin, 1972.

Simkin, William E. *Mediation and the Dynamics of Collective Bargaining.* Washington, D. C.: Bureau of National Affairs, 1971.

Index